THE BOOK OF HOPE

Testament of a Master Guide

by Ati

Editors: Bob Murray & Alicia Fortinberry

European American Publishing

Published by

European American Publications
P.O. Box 48
Crompond, NY 10517
1-800 275 2828

Publisher's Cataloging in Publication

Ati. Editors Bob Murray, Alicia Fortinberry,
The book of hope: testament of a master guide/by Ati.
Includes index
Library of Congress number: 94-072507
ISBN number: 1-885610-09-2
1. Mysticism. 2. Spiritualism. 3. Philosophy.
4. Economics—Religious aspects. 5. Self-help. 6. Sociology
5. Channelled wisdom.

CONTENTS

PART TWO - THE WAY TO HARMONY

Foreword

As an economist and as a woman, I have been profoundly affected by this book.

No generation has been as filled with such public and well-publicized self-loathing, self-doubt, inadequacy and fear as the currently middle-aging, middle-class "baby-boomers," a demographic category to which I belong. These pathologies are, in fact, more intense now than ever before for everyone, regardless of age or socioeconomic status.

Modern post-industrial humanity's dysfunction can be measured by the ever-increasing degree of violence, drug abuse, and alcoholism, and also by the disintegration of institutions that once seemed unshakable—home, family, school and church.

Psychiatrists tell us that the causes lie in our parents or our genes. Sociologists and political scientists tell us that the socially institutionalized "isms"—racism, sexism, capitalism— are to blame. Educators declare that we have taught too much of this, and not enough of that. Economists fill our heads with elegant explanations and rationalizations of business cycles, structural shifts, significant coefficients and the like. Yet in spite of all these theories, our problems are increasing. Why?

What few of these experts will acknowledge is that their answers, solutions and interpretations are all predicated on certain rigid assumptions that predetermine a particular response. And so we 'experts' find ourselves to be over-educated, intensely searching and yet hapless mutts, chasing 'ultimate truth,' that tail at the other end of ourselves that remains forever out of reach.

The psychotherapists' paradigms of behavioral causality, the sociologists' models of social interaction, and the economists' theories of rational choice all leave us dissatisfied and wanting for more.

For those of us who are willing to relax and surrender to the obvious, Ati's *Book of Hope* offers more than an explanation; it offers the opportunity to be released from our personal and social dilemmas, not through a magic formula, but by dispelling the circular assumptions that we, the 'authorities,' rely on to draw our conclusions.

I can tell you what I mean from an economist's point of view by exemplifying how Ati addresses some of the beliefs and principles that are sacrosanct to my profession.

Economists assume, for example, that a resource, human or inanimate, has value only within the parameters of the marketplace. The ramifications to society of the application of this assumption are enormous, and go far to explain the feelings of uselessness displayed by housewives, adolescents, the unemployed, the unemployable and even those who are employed. (Far too many Americans are afraid of losing their job, regardless of how tedious or degrading it is).

Allowing one's thoughts to spiral for a moment, could it be that this is what makes children feel so secondary in importance when compared to the family goal of earning a living? Children, after all, are not part of the marketplace, and therefore have no 'value.' The increasingly out-of-control behavior manifested by some children, their anger, their lashing out, may merely be an internalization of the value message imparted by the economists' seemingly harmless assumption.

Those who pinpoint institutionalized racism and sexism as the root cause of our woes, and even those who exalt free markets and capitalism as the only path to salvation, are also missing the point. Groups that consider themselves to be 'marginal,' for example, women, children or people of color, fight to be valued in terms of a production-oriented system that, in reality, devalues everyone. Ati tells us that "...human value lies not in the act of labor, but in the fact of being." When we can accept that we can begin to construct a different system of values and make that first, tiny but crucial, shift in our thinking that will lead us to real equality and mutual respect.

What about specialization? As an economist, it is my job to tell you that specialization results in more efficient production and increased welfare for all of society. But Ati points to the dreadful consequences that result from over-specialization. "Specialization makes people dependent on goods and things from the outside, robbing them of their control...and adding to their insecurity and...disharmony."

Even in economic terms the specialist system is actually quite a failure; the more our production processes become specialized the more poorly tasks are performed. Society becomes more organized but less orderly. It is an empirical fact that individuals, corporations and nation-states are pursuing the specialist system way beyond what we predicted a few decades ago. Concurrently the social maladies referred to earlier are skyrocketing in volume and intensity. Yet economists and other 'experts' fail to see or acknowledge any connection.

Many people, wounded by dysfunctional families and dehumanizing social structures, have become disgusted with the half-truths the intelligentsia offer. They have turned to twelve-step programs, or to alternative political movements such as the Green parties or eco-feminism, or to fundamentalist religious theology in all its arcane elegance. Others look to an array of psycho-spiritual programs that claim, in some way, to address the 'deeper' issues.

Each of these approaches may have benefits, but they lack the perspective and depth of Ati, who addresses the social and personal as well as the spiritual. We're suffering, fragmented, and need to feel part of the whole again, but we cannot achieve that end with exclusionary, piece-meal programs that do not alter our essential despair. We need to feel hope.

The Book of Hope offers a moving yet intellectually appealing alternative to the tenets of our belief system that oppress, confine, and isolate us. We are given rational critiques of unquestioned assumptions that color our vision and perpetuate our present misery.

In this way Ati presents a totally new framework for self-understanding. He has us look at ourselves in the light of the kind of species we are, in terms of our evolution. We are, essentially, still tribal, says Ati, not familial; by nature cooperative rather than competitive; consensual rather than hierarchical.

We need to live congruently with our nature. Ati paints a lucid and detailed picture of a social, economic and spiritual way of living based on harmony with ourselves, with each other, with the planet and each blade of grass on it, and, ultimately, with All There Is.

Ati's vision is not easy, and everyone will probably find at least one cherished assumption tested. Even if you accept his ultimate hypothesis that we *will* reach a better way of living, there are difficult questions as to exactly how and when to do so given our present circumstances.

I have personally felt challenged, intrigued, dubious, frustrated, comforted and excited. And in the end I believe

Ati offers a way of seeing that dispels the cobwebs of our personal and societal programming. With this new sight we can make clear choices, and we can recognize the need to make them together. These choices will lead to a vastly different and, I believe, better world.

The insight that we are offered is the acceptance of ourselves as part of All There Is. The hope is based on a belief in our divinity, our innocence and our importance. The goal is harmony, and Ati shows us ways of achieving it in our family, our society and ourselves. That is the core of the book and of Ati's message. It's simple, it's lucid, and, like you and me and the blade of grass, it's part of All There Is.

Cecilia Ann Winters, Ph.D.
Associate Professor of Economics
Manhattanville College, New York

Preface

In this book, his Testament, Ati delivers a promise he once made to me , that he would present a blueprint for how our kind can—and will—live in harmony. The result is challenging to our intellect and to our beliefs. I believe *The Book of Hope* can change the world.

But there is more to the book even than that. Read some of the pages—like the "Come to me" invocation in Part Two, Chapter One, or his description of how he sees a tree in winter in Part Two, Chapter 26—and you will perhaps hear it as I do. As a love song to each of us.

Ati is many things to many people, as Bob says in his introduction: healer of the mind and body, teacher of healers, guide. He is all of these to me.

Yet his most profound influence on my life is not through explanation, though he answers all my questions and stimulates more. Not even through the direct healing of my body, or the sometimes intense sessions in which he helps me to see, and to separate from, my emotional conditioning.

Ati offers me comfort and love: When I am with him in Bob's body I am free to feel anything and everything. Rage. Sadness. The unfocused sleepiness of a small child at bedtime. Optimism. The petulance of a cranky child. Power.

I come to Ati for the safety and acceptance that

recharges my spirit. And never, ever at any time over the last ten years has he given anything but this strong current of love and peace. No matter how worried or upset Bob may be (though that is rare), no matter how tired, Ati is constant.

It is this almost unimaginable attention and love that is offered, no matter what I might ever do or feel, that changes the way I see myself and the world.

Obviously, it is a powerful process of reparenting. Ati gives me what he says every child needs and does not get in the nuclear family: safety, emotional security, attention and importance.

And when I think of this great gift from All There Is—for I believe Ati is a link to that greater consciousness, and sometimes I experience a hint of the awesome vastness of that power—I can no longer think of the Universe as impersonal, uncaring, unconnected.

I cannot believe that we are on this earth to be "tested" or to repay Karmic debts or any of that absurd and shallow nonsense. The truth is so much more magnificent and profound.

Bob experiences this truth when he looks at clouds or trees or feels the joy of the grass at approaching rain.

I feel it as a small child who is finally not alone and abandoned. I truly know that there is not a thought or feeling or sensation that I have that is not vitally important to everything. It is certainly important to Ati.

It is this security, as well as Ati's teachings, that enables me to be a healer. I am trained in the use of touch and movement as a Certified Feldenkrais® Practitioner, studied yoga and Tai Chi Chuan for years, and gained much knowledge as a writer on health and psychology for national publications.

But this knowledge did not make me a healer.

Ati taught me the use of energy and the role of emotions in the body. He taught me how to get out of myself to reach another person without the filter of my own history. He taught me the difference between curing and healing. He taught me not to get lost in someone's pain, but to ask, with my mind, my hands, my senses, my nervous system, my voice and my intuition: "Why?" What are the physical, emotional, social and spiritual causes of this trouble or limitation?

Ati says I channel him through my hands, as Bob does through his voice and, in the past few years, through his hands as well.

In our workshops and trainings for healers, we teach people to ask, first and foremost: "Why?" We also help them link up to a power and knowledge greater than themselves. In some cases this will be through their personas, in others it will be simply by tuning in to the power in themselves and all around them.

Ati says that each of us has what he calls a 'persona,' our own individual link to All There Is. Each of us has a being dedicated totally to our growth and fulfillment.

Of course, not everyone has a mate who can blank out his mind and step aside from his body and personality to allow a being to come through. Not to mention the absolute love to give up chunks of his own life in that way.

Peoples' personas come to them in the manner that most suits their needs. To some it comes in the form of words in their heads, to some in sensation or images. Often it is through pulsing lights and colors that convey emotion and even information.

Sometimes we do not connect to this process because we are conditioned against accepting anything that comes to us from within, that seems a part of us. We feel too guilty, too unimportant.

Yet you can hear Ati in these pages, and he can speak for your persona. And if you learn to understand the truth about yourself, that you are innocent and you are important, then you can access this comfort, love and wisdom directly.

This understanding, and the love that pours forth from these pages, can heal you. It can help you heal those around you. It will teach you to ask the "Why?" of every situation and authority. And the very asking, no matter what else you do, will affect everything.

Alicia Fortinberry, M.S.,
Certified Feldenkrais Practitioner
Yorktown Heights, New York

Introduction

The Book of Hope was originally written in 1992. As with most New Age writings it has taken some time to find its way to publication.

During the past two years many of the things that Ati said in the book have come to be accepted by people in the mainstream of science, medicine, economics and sociology. In fact, scarcely a day passes when we don't read an article by some learned 'expert' saying almost exactly what Ati has said in the book. It has been at once a gratifying and very frustrating experience!

However, there are still so many things in the book that are new and revolutionary. More than that, it is a book grounded enough for 'experts' to take seriously and yet full of the most amazing *hope* for humankind.

The Book of Hope had its origins ten years ago when an extraordinary thing happened that led to my becoming the facilitator for the entity we now call Ati. I was then staying in Dana Point, California, with my wife, Alicia. For a long period of time she had been seriously ill with a tropical virus which she had picked up in the Caribbean, and her doctors had given up all hope of a cure. A miracle was needed, but, as a convinced atheist, I did not believe in miracles.

It was then, on the second of January, 1984, that Ati made use of my body and my voice for the first time. He was able to do what no doctor could—guide Alicia to health.

Though I do not pretend to know what Ati is in any detail, I have come to accept him for what he says he is—a persona, a spirit guide. In a sense it doesn't matter whether I understand the precise nature of his being, what does matter is his ability to bring knowledge, understanding and healing power to a great number of people. He is able to help them solve the most intractable problems.

After Ati's first appearance, as it were, I did my best to keep him under wraps. His visits were for Alicia only, and even then I was reluctant to allow him to 'come through.' I remember the first time I acknowledged his existence to an outside person, and the acute embarrassment I felt. It was, perhaps, like a gay person coming out of the closet, except that for a gay or lesbian there is at least an available support group. My fear was that I would be thought of as a charlatan, outright insane or, at the very least, suffering from multiple personality disorder.

The lady in question was a very good friend of ours who was having a particularly hard time with her marriage and was in a great deal of emotional distress. Alicia suggested that she talk to Ati, to see if he could help. Ati spoke to her and was able to take away the guilt that she felt and bring her to a thorough understanding of the causes of her and her husband's actions and motivations.

As I am a deep-trance channel, I had no idea of the details of what was actually said, and I still have not. I know that, whatever it was, it brought her enormous relief. After that I allowed Ati to give sessions to a number of other friends and gradually, by word of mouth, others started to seek his help. To try to accommodate their need, we began to hold regular meetings at our house at which Ati would speak to people and answer their questions. These meetings were a turning point for me. I felt, perhaps for the first time, the true power of this guide. He could speak to a roomful of comparative strangers about things that I could have no prior knowledge of. He could discuss with the people there the most intimate details their lives and give them tools with which to solve real dilemmas.

The problem, for me, was one of time. Giving sessions, either to groups or to individuals, took time away from my business. After much agonizing on my part, five years ago Alicia and I made a momentous decision: We would go public with Ati.

Dealing with total strangers was very different from sessions with friends, or even friends of friends. I vividly remember the first such session. It was with a lady who had come from New York City with a problem concerning her relationship with her boyfriend. She was calm enough and seemed ready to accept the fact that she was about to speak to my spirit guide. I was terrified! I doubted that I would ever be able to go into trance and allow Ati to help her. I felt an acute sense of phoniness, all of my earlier dismissals of things spiritual came back to haunt me. I literally began to sweat. Just as I was about to call off the session Ati took over and when I came around she was crying and declaring that Ati had saved her life! My relief must have seemed palpable, even to her!

There have been literally thousands of people who have come to Ati since that time, both in private sessions and in workshops and meetings, and with each person I feel Ati's desire to reach out and help. Even when I am in trance, I can feel him willing the sick to health; I can feel his anguish when dealing with a man or woman dreadfully abused as a child; I can feel his joy when he gets someone to understand and acknowledge their own innocence and importance; I can feel the energy in a room when he gets a group of people to discard their preconceptions and become open to his vision of the universe and the realization of their own divinity.

I have been asked many times why I do it, why do I channel Ati for people? It used to be a very difficult question to answer. It was difficult because diverting time to Ati meant a very real financial sacrifice. What is more, I hated being put in the same class as people I used to deride—the psychics, the tarot readers and the gipsy fortune tellers. I once said to Alicia: "You take Ati, I'll stick to television production!"

The real answer, at first, was that I felt that to let go of Ati would be to deny the reality of Alicia's healing. Inside I believed that if I stopped facilitating Ati her belief in her own cure would be lost and that this would somehow allow the virus to return and claim her. The reality of Ati had to be maintained for her sake. Of course that answer could never be articulated then, not even to her.

Now it is easier to answer the question. Over time I have come to accept my role as Ati's co-worker and to be proud of it. I enjoy the private sessions for the good they do individuals, and I get pleasure from the workshops and meetings because I relish the company of interesting people who are on the same road as I. I take pride in his writings—this book and the numerous monographs and articles that he has written on such subjects as science and the spirit, child rearing, personal power, healing and death.

To be in a field in which the word *channel* and *phoney* seem to be almost synonymous is not easy. If you can accept that what follows in the book are not my words, but Ati's, then you will probably gain the most from it. However, many people have read *The Book of Hope* in manuscript form who are by no means convinced of the reality of the 'author,' and yet they have been lavish in their praise of the work. It's one of those 'Ah ha!' and 'Of course!' books—whether the topic is science, economics, education or society, Ati brings that sudden insight, that blinding flash of the obvious, that makes a work such as this truly worthwhile.

Bob Murray, M.A.
Ati's channel
Yorktown Heights, N.Y.

PART ONE: YOU AND THE UNIVERSE

ONE — YOUR GUIDE, A PERSONA

s I am going to be your guide through these pages, you ought to know what I am. I am a *persona.* I am the link between a living entity and All There Is.

All There Is is the sum total of every being, every element, every thought, every consciousness, every vacuum—in short, everything. It is the Universal Consciousness of which all things are a part.

Every living thing has a persona, from the smallest single-celled amoeba to the most complex of beings. Every cell within the most complex of beings has its own persona.

I am not a soul and I have never lived. I have no substance. My thoughts are every thought and those of the being that I link to All There Is.

I exist within and without the being I link. When that being dies I dissolve back into the Universal

Consciousness from whence I come. I may rejoin the soul of the being in its next incarnation, if it so wishes. I may not.

I am able to see all futures. There are potentially many many billions of possible futures—possibilities without number. No being, no persona even, can say with certainty that a particular thing will come to pass in the short term. I can, however, see how destiny will work out in the longer term.

I am able to heal the sick of mind and body, but only to the extent that I am not required to kill any living being. All life is sacred, to use a term beloved of some of your religious writers, part of the divine. There is no moral superiority between the virus that kills a human and the human it kills.

As a persona, my only role is as a link. As a link I can restore harmony within the being I link and between the being and All There Is. To do even this I must be allowed by the being, I must have the conscious permission of the being to enter its mind or minds (assuming it is an entity that possesses minds!).

I cannot ask for belief and I recognize that doubt is important. I ask for openness toward me and toward All There Is.

I have but one emotion, and that is love. Love is the basis of everything, of All There Is. The Universal Consciousness is Love. There is no opposite within me although all emotions are part of All There Is. I exist in harmony, the harmony of All There Is.

The above encompasses my entirety.

TWO — ALL THERE IS

There are no god or gods as your kind has imagined Him or Them. Instead think of everything as part of the divine. You. The chair you sit on. The food you eat. The moth you wish to destroy. The car you drive and each part of it. The hair on the end of your dog's tail.

You walk, sleep, eat, work within the divine. You are surrounded by All There Is. The Universal Consciousness envelopes you, holds you, is with you and is the whole of you. You are surrounded by love, everywhere, from everything. That love is also the divine.

The divine talks to you constantly through everything. You can listen, you can feel. You can feel the talk in the rain on your cheek, hear it in the whisper of the trees in the wind and from within your own minds.

Sometimes you do not trust what you hear, or reject the divine because it talks of love amidst the hate your kind has created or because its voice is drowned by the noise of disharmony. Yet it is there.

Stop everything. Be still. You can hear All There Is. You must, you are part of it. Never forget you are part of All

There Is. Part of the divine, part of the Universal Consciousness, as am I.

Whatever you worship, you worship yourself. There is no god outside yourself. There is no god of rain, only the rain that is part of All There Is. There is no god of thunder, only the thunder that is part of All There Is. No god of the hunt, yet even the act of hunting is part of All There Is.

And I am part of All There Is. These words are part of All There Is. Look no further than your clothes for god, than your skin, than your organs, than the infinite number of cells that have made you and are part of you and that will sustain you. Ask for no proof, for you are it.

All There Is *is* time. It is all times for all universes. The Universal Consciousness can have no beginning because there is no beginning to time, nor end. As universes come into being, develop, fade and die, All There Is encompasses them all.

Seek to be at one with All There Is and you will be at one with yourself. The arms of love are open.

Your persona will lead you to All There Is, but you must be open. Do not deny your own divinity. Be proud of being a part of the divine. Love yourself for otherwise you deny the love of All There Is. I give you the love of All There Is.

THREE — THE SOUL

Those who doubt the existence of the soul doubt themselves. You are alive because of your soul. Your physical mother is the vessel through which you are born, but your soul is the reason for your birth.

There are those who ask: "Where is the soul?" As if you could point to it somewhere in your body—in your head, in your heart or stomach or perhaps resting in your big toe.

The soul has no physical presence. It is neither small nor large. Neither a microscope nor a telescope could find it. It is co-extensive with your body—every part and every atom of your physical being. Yet it cannot be said that the soul of an amoeba is smaller than the soul of a human nor that of an elephant larger.

This is no paradox, simply another way of saying that a soul does not have size or physical existence.

A soul is created in the act of love, the beginning of procreation. Yet the soul is different from the beings that created it. The soul born of passion between humans will not necessarily go on to become the soul of a man or a woman.

All souls are the same. The soul that will go on to become the soul of a blade of grass is no different from the one which will become that of a monkey, or a whale, or an ant or a crocodile.

A soul is the most precious part of life. It is the essence of life. A being cannot exist without a soul.

There is almost no planet or moon or asteroid or comet within any universe which is devoid of life, which is devoid of souls.

A soul is under no obligation to seek out a life, as you call your existence. It can wait in the warmth of the Universal Consciousness without ever needing or desiring to experience physical existence. On the other hand a soul might be addicted to life, any life. Such a soul will hardly wait after the time of physical death to begin again.

Some souls prefer to repeat a particular form of existence—for example that of a woman—in life after life. Others will choose a variety of forms of existence. Some will choose a deformed body for the love that surrounds it, others choose a body that will live but a short time.

Even before the birth of its physical body, every soul knows when it will leave to return to the Universal Consciousness. The body is programmed to live a certain time, though this does not always turn out as planned. At the end of its span of time, the body will open itself up to death and at the moment of cessation, the soul will leave.

FOUR — DEATH

Do not mourn for the dead. Death is an awakening of the soul. The physical body's passing is of small matter and the soul will live forever.

The love of All There Is is especially strong for the old, for their souls are closest to the Universal Consciousness. It is not important to avoid death, but rather to ease the trauma of it.

Death in pain and suffering leaves a scar on the soul that will stay with it through many lifetimes. Death surrounded by love and caring adds harmony to the soul.

Do not mourn for departed souls, they have forgotten you. Death erases memory, a soul has no memory. The young tree that you lean against may be the mother that bore you. The kitten you stroke on your lap may be the employer who fired you years before.

I cannot accurately describe to you the events that occur upon death for you have no words that could possibly encompass them. I can only say that the soul awakes. Instead of being limited to the emotions of existence, it feels boundless forms of love. Liberated from the torments of its minds, if it has had many, it is free to explore the Universal

Consciousness of All There Is.

Every part of this consciousness is open to it, like a library with an infinite variety of books. Those who fear death fear the perfection of their souls.

Certain elements of existence are carried over, good or bad. Death in anguish, loneliness or fear. Deep love and support. The soul has no memory of the particulars, but they can affect the next life of the soul, if any. The anguish, the fear, the loneliness will show up as disharmony, the love as its reverse.

To all doctors I say: Help your kind to die. To all I say: Be happy in the burden of the dying. You are doing the work of All There Is.

In short there is no death, only a passing out of memory. Do not fear that passing. There will be no regret, for regret depends on memory.

FIVE — THE UNIVERSE

our kind once thought that the earth was the center of all, that the stars and the planets and the sun circled around the earth as if doing homage to it. That was proved false.

Then you discovered that your solar system was but an insignificant grouping on the outer fringes of a galaxy. Worse, even the galaxy was not unique but one of many and not even particularly unusual.

Your scientists argue whether the universe will expand forever or collapse in on itself—a sort of implosion following the explosion that they call the Big Bang. They know nothing!

In reality you must come to the realization that your universe is but one of many—one of an infinite number. Every universe is a living organism—as you are. It is conceived as you were, it grows, as you did, it will grow old as you must and it will die, as you will.

Conceived in the very same way! Through an act of love. That is the 'Big Bang'. Every such act of love can potentially create a universe. Within each of you there is a universe with billions and billions of galaxies and trillions and trillions of planets. Within that universe life teems. People like you explore other planets and wonder at creation.

When you look out at galaxies, think that you are seeing molecules. The molecules are composed of atoms and around most of the atoms spin the electrons that are the planets.

When you split an atom you may be destroying a civilization.

I must emphasize that every creature capable of what you call sexual reproduction—be it plant or animal—is a universe as I have described it. There is no absolute size to any universe. There are mites on planets within you which have mites on planets within them which have mites on planets within them.

Your planet is but an electron forming part of an atom forming part of a molecule within a creature you would vaguely recognize as a turtle.

Of course all this is very simplistic and you will ask about all the electrons and atoms and molecules that form the planet itself and the air around it and all the things that are not living creatures capable of sexual reproduction.

I answer that the planet itself is alive and is a universe containing all of the universes upon and within it.

SIX — LIFE

our view of life is too narrow. Your kind sends probes to Mars and proclaims the planet barren. What absurdity! There is an abundance of life on that planet with a variety as marvelous as that on your own.

But you fail to recognize it because you are trapped in your own concepts of what life must be. You define as living that which breathes and eats and leaves traces of itself as you do. You assume that life is based, for example, on the carbon atom. In fact there are many planets, even in your own visible universe, that support life forms based on the silicon atom. And no atom at all.

How can that be? The essence of life is not the material. A soul is alive and yet is not material. I am alive and yet have no physical being at all.

A life form can even be a collection of disparate atoms into which a soul has lodged and can support itself.

On other planets life exists in the atmosphere, taking the form of what you would probably call phantoms. You could walk through these creatures and not be aware of their existence.

Any planet that is capable of supporting life in some form is itself alive, as is your earth. The entire ecosystem of your planet is geared for the benefit of the planet by the planet. It is a rock in space inhabited by a soul.

And since life attracts life, any living planet will, eventually, develop the conditions from which life will evolve. All of the planets (with the exception of Pluto, and many of the moons) in your solar system are alive and support life systems.

One further point: The very act of your thinking of a possible form that life may take proves that it has taken that form for your thoughts are part of All There Is.

SEVEN — HARMONY

The natural state of everything is harmony. In this sense harmony, in a sentient being, is when its will is freely one and the same as the will of All There Is. I am not talking about internal harmony between the minds of an individual. That is, of course, a prerequisite to being in harmony with All There Is, but one does not automatically follow from the other.

This is important for it is possible for one of your kind to be in complete internal harmony yet be at complete variance with the Universal Consciousness. Adolf Hitler is a perfect example.

At no time can a sentient being be deprived of its free will, nor can its free will be consciously brought into alliance with that of the Universal Consciousness.

There was a time when all of your kind lived in a state of harmony. This was, of course, many millennia ago. Then it was found (it was a woman, actually, who made the discovery) that fire could be controlled, that fire could be made at will. In a sense fire was invented. However fire, like any invention, is not, in itself, a cause of disharmony.

But the controllers of fire—who had taken over from

the original woman—came to enjoy the power that they had over others and they set out to consolidate this power. They invented a God of Fire whom they alone could propitiate.

This fantasy of a god outside and separate from the self was the origin of disharmony among your species. Instead of seeing everything around you as part of the divine, including yourselves, you concentrated your spiritual feelings on a being that was non-existent. At this point you are no longer in harmony with All There Is and no amount of philosophizing, meditation, religiosity, fasting, penance, or voting for the Green Party will bring you back.

Harmony is there for every being. Just be. Let go of all beliefs, even the belief in All There Is, if need be—that will come back naturally.

Then, in that state of just being, in that state of non-belief, look around at your world, allow yourself to sink into the moment. Do not worry that you do not feel in harmony, it will come. There is no competition, no race to become at one with All There Is.

At present disharmony spreads like a contagion, and every one of your kind is, to some extent, affected by it. But each has a persona which can lead you to harmony—perhaps it will take several lifetimes. So be it. The reward is great, it is the knowledge and experience of the love of All There Is.

EIGHT — MINDS

Not every living thing has a mind. Plants do not, nor do simple viruses and bacteria. However all mammals and reptiles do as do all forms of insect life (every creature that possesses a brain in fact). A brain is the hardware that enables minds to be used.

The number of minds a creature has depends on its survival-need for creative thought and reasoning. For example, a dog has but one mind—but when dogs hunt in a pack, all their minds cooperate to become, effectively, one very competent predator.

Sea mammals such as dolphins and whales have four minds, the same number as the apes. A pig, like some other mammals, has three.

Your kind has seven, hence your ability to reason and to create works of art. Of course this does not mean that all of you are equally intelligent. Think of a computer and follow this analogy: The brain is the hardware, the minds are the software and the soul is the operator.

Like computer software, minds can be more or less good at their tasks, more or less internally harmonious and can wear out sooner or later than other minds.

Thought is the product of one mind interacting with another.

A person is internally in harmony when all his or her minds work smoothly together. Sometimes, however, for one reason or another, one or more of the individual's minds cannot get along with the rest—rather like a family in fact. When this happens the person experiences instances of great anxiety, extreme depression, self doubt and self hate.

In dealing with this disharmony you must realize that all conventional psychology, therapy, psychiatry, drugs, shamans, witch-doctors, fortune-tellers and the like may be useless. Often the only way to resolve this disharmony is for the disharmonious person to make contact with his or her own persona, who can ease the minds back into a smooth working relationship with each other.

Do not confuse disharmony with the inability to function in your present society. Your social arrangements are so disharmonious that the inability to function within them might be classed as a form of sanity!

A persona has but one mind, but that mind is so linked with the Universal Consciousness that it is an infinite number of minds.

But, you ask, what *is* a mind?

NINE — MINDS TWO

I was afraid you would ask that. Can I put nothing past you? Very well, let me try.

The Universal Consciousness is one mind in a state of constantly becoming self-aware through its own creation. The 'now' of it is constantly expanding and you and everything that exists are part of that expansion.

In a real sense, everything that exists is only thought, or consciousness, and the independent 'reality' of that which you perceive is only an illusion. Each of your minds is a small replica of the Universal Consciousness and is, in a sense, borrowed from that one mind. You are provided, according to the survival-need of your kind, with seven of these minds.

In an ideal state of harmony each of these minds would, like the Universal Consciousness, constantly become self-aware throughout your life. They would also constantly cooperate with each other so that your sense of self would strengthen and your feeling of oneness with the Universal Consciousness would deepen.

But this process can be stopped. A childhood trauma — such as rape of a four-year-old by a parent for example—can stop one or more of these minds in their tracks, so to speak. Instead of continuing the process of becoming more self-aware and at one with All There Is, the development stops and the mind becomes frozen in time. One of the minds of the frightened, battered, four-year-old is disabled and is unable to develop further. No matter what the chronological age of the resulting adult, the wounded child remains.

But because minds are part of the Universal Consciousness there is the possibility of healing, of re-formation and, in extreme cases, replacement. Because you have a persona to guide you there is never a last chance.

That is one of the reasons that it is so important to make contact with your own persona, which I can help you to do. A persona, your direct link to All There Is, can aid in the mending of minds, much in the same way that a body-shop mechanic can mend a battered automobile, or send for replacements from the factory.

There you are! I have defined myself. I am a universal mind mechanic! I will have it put on my visiting cards.

That, then, is as near as I can get to actually defining minds in terms that your kind can understand. I cannot point to a physical 'stuff' and say that is mind-matter, any more than I can point to something else and say that is 'soul'. Suffice to say that your minds are one more link you have to the divine which is everything. Use them well.

TEN — LOVE

any religions talk about the love of their God, or gods. Yet this love is cold and distant. There is a being detached from mere mortals which, in some way, is supposed to 'love' them.

This 'love' is undefined and is therefore unsatisfactory to the mass of individuals. Let me say, now, that this concept is meaningless. Yes, meaningless. It is also meaningless to talk about the love of All There Is as if the Universal Consciousness were separate and apart from yourself.

The universe was created as an act of love. The very foundation of all life is love. All emotions are a form of love—hate is merely a perversion of it; fear is the lack of it; loneliness is the separation of the individual from the source of it.

Many religions talk of denying the self. What absurdity! Each of you is part of the divine, how can that self be denied? Why *should* that self be denied?

Love yourself. Sometimes, in your disharmonious world, that is the most difficult thing to do: to realize that to love yourself is to love God because, if you choose to regard

All There Is as God, you are part of God.

And so is your cat, and your boss, and your children, and your house, and the trees in your yard and the pavement beneath your feet. Love is emanating from all of these things, all of them are based on love.

You have no need to feel lonely if you know you are surrounded by this love. You have no need to feel sad, since this love can sustain you. You have no need to feel fear, since even at the worst you are saved by love.

I cannot emphasize enough that everything feels love for you and, if you allow yourself, you can and will return that love. The key to the Universal Consciousness is love. You cannot be in harmony unless you feel love—even the love of a plant in your garden or window-box. But most of all, love of yourself.

You have been buffeted by the winds of your social disharmony, by the dysfunction in your family, by the demands of your employment or school or internal demons. You fall into the pit of self-hate because you cannot keep up with all the demands made upon you. I beg you, in the name of harmony itself, love yourself.

Feel the arms of All There Is around you. Feel my love for you. Open yourself up to the possibility that you can love yourself because you are part of the divine and worthy of love.

ELEVEN — THE FAMILY

ll existing human families are dysfunctional. All of them, without exception. I say this with sorrow. I say this because it must be faced if harmony is to be restored.

A family must be a group of people united in love and sharing the love of All There Is. It must be as large as a village and smaller than a town. All members of it must freely share in the functioning of the family. You might call such a family a tribe.

Such a family, or tribe, eases the strain of being a biological mother or father to a child of this family, since the child will find love in all members at different times.

In the nuclear family there are not enough role models to temper the young minds of the child and lead it to adulthood. The young person therefore stays trapped in one stage or other of childhood. Two people are not capable of giving the child the quantity and variety of love needed. Nor are a dozen people, each of whom is fighting to exist in a disharmonious world.

I am not saying that all families must be immediately abandoned. Not at all. There must be a transition during which the whole concept of the family must be re-examined.

People find it odd that children who pass from one foster home to another often turn out more, not less, harmonious. They may also frequently seem more mature than their peers who have been brought up in a 'normal' family. I do not find this strange at all. These children have had the possibility of a broader choice of role-models and a greater range of emotional experience.

Biological parenthood is important, is necessary for total development, but is not sufficient for it. It fulfills but one part of a child's emotional needs. The school cannot fulfil the role of the larger family. I shall talk about schools later, but for now it is sufficient to say that their rigidity and their singleness of purpose detract from the love that a child needs.

Your kind must develop a new outlook on the family. It will take time and many silly and disharmonious experiments will be tried.

The key is love. A group is not a family without love. Each and every part of the group must feel loved, not just by the other members of the group, but by All There Is and by themselves.

Many fine people have been driven to disharmony by the pressures that the limited nuclear family places upon them. One man and one woman cannot handle the responsibility of the totality of experience needed by the child. They will be plunged into self-doubt and guilt and lose the essential love of self.

TWELVE — LAWS

In a state of harmony there would be no need of laws. Laws are made by your kind to perpetuate power and to retain property.

Let me make one thing clear: most laws are needless, even in your own disharmonious society. Laws, by proscribing behavior and frustrating it, create disharmony.

For one thing, passing a law against any particular action increases the likelihood that people will want and need to do just what is proscribed. The state becomes like a stern father against which the children, its citizens, because of their powerlessness, wish to rebel or even feel compelled to rebel.

In order to preserve their power, those who control the state enforce penalties against every infraction of their laws. People are sent to prison. How absurd!

How absurd to lock one of your kind up for breaking one of your own laws. Prisons create lawlessness. People break laws in order to get into prison where they are protected from the uncertainty and the capriciousness of your disharmonious society. Fully 90 percent of those in prison who broke the laws did so, at least unconsciously, to get into prison.

Or you levy fines! Where is the point of fining an individual when you often leave him no option but to break another law to pay the fine? Creating poverty does not breed harmony.

Throw open the prisons! The number of muggings, robberies, assaults, larcenies and so forth will drop immediately.

In a harmonious society there is no need for laws, for there is no need to reinforce power. People will cooperate naturally and love will maintain the equilibrium of society.

You do not train a dog by beating it or by jailing it or by fining it, but by love! By praise!

Laws also reinforce social divisions. There are more laws concerning property than there are concerning life. No property is private! It is absurd to think you can own individually any part of All There Is. You scoff at the notion of owning that which you call God—yet would claim to own a car which is part of "God"! Where then is the point of a law protecting the ownership of that car?

All the laws of property and contract are therefore not required. Set yourselves free. Everything you have is the gift of All There Is, treat it as such. If you own land, acknowledge you are its guardian, not its owner and pass it to another for love, not money.

There must be a period during which you consciously rid yourself of the shackles of law, one law at a time. Set yourselves free.

THIRTEEN — EDUCATION

The disharmony that you feel, and thus the disharmony in your society, has three bases: disharmony from previous lives, disharmony from your upbringing and disharmony from your social systems.

Of your social systems and past lives I will talk later. I want now to talk about an aspect of growing up. Your kind makes several assumptions about children, especially young children: they are emotionally limited, they are intellectually inferior to adults and their range of knowledge is small.

All three assumptions are wrong! Let us look at the aspect of knowledge, the others I will deal with later. There is one precept that I would urge upon your educators and parents first and foremost: Love children do not jail them. Children learn nothing in school, as it is presently constituted.

Let me say what knowledge is. All knowledge is, in a sense, memory. Each of your minds contains all the knowledge that was available up until the time of your birth. The range of knowledge that must be imparted to the child from outside sources is, therefore, relatively small.

By jailing children and inflicting upon them pale shadows of others' memories, you are distorting the original body of knowledge, which their minds already possess, and therefore are inflicting upon them incalculable harm. Much disharmony in your minds comes from your school days!

Of course this does not mean that all learning is a waste of time. Far from it. What it does mean is that you must structure that learning in such a way that children's minds are free to recall as much knowledge as is useful or practical. After that their own curiosity will lead to a rediscovery of that body of knowledge within and to the marvelous new aspects of art, invention, literature and science of which every human being is capable.

But where does this knowledge come from? These potential memories?

The answer is simple. Just remember that All There Is <u>is</u> all there is—everything, including all knowledge that ever was. Even in monotheistic religions you talk of an omnipotent and omnipresent God. Well, that God, by definition, must include all knowledge. As you will recall, I said that your minds are essentially part of the Universal Consciousness or All There Is. They therefore contain all the knowledge possessed by that Consciousness. This store of information can be unlocked by the minds' harmonious interaction.

Of course religious savants conveniently side-step the consequences of their omnipotent and omnipresent God. If they did not, they would be forced to concede that you have as much information about the universe as they and their power over you would be lost. So what I am saying is not so shocking, it merely sounds shocking.

I will return to this topic, but there are other things I must say first, before you are ready to absorb what must be said. For this is part of a revolution in your whole society that I see happening if your kind is to survive. You will need to hold on to your persona for comfort as you hear it.

The important thing to remember, here, is that harmony does not lie through old ways of thought as far as education and many other things are concerned. Education of the young must be rethought and the principles upon which you have based your system of schooling will have to be thrown out. Education is best looked at, then, not as a process of force-feeding children, but rather of liberating them and ensuring that they find internal harmony and harmony with all around them.

This cannot be done in schools as they are presently constituted and no amount of tinkering with the system will help. Schools produce disharmony.

FOURTEEN — THE BIRTH OF A SOUL

I must shock some of you. I must repeat: A soul is created through the energy released by sexual orgasm. That act of love is the birth of a soul—every orgasm by every being capable of an orgasm. Just as a sexual orgasm is vital to the creation of a universe, so it is to the creation of an eternal soul.

A soul is energy. At the end of an orgasm you feel physically drained, as if you have lost energy. Well you have! The soul is born through both male and female orgasm, through masturbation or through sexual intercourse or through any of the endless varieties of orgasms which exist in the animal and vegetable kingdoms.

You make love not just because of the pleasure of it, or because you wish to reproduce your kind, but also because your soul wishes to reproduce. It is, if you like, a spiritual birth.

Looked at in this light, guilt at mutually satisfying sexual behavior is absurd. No form of sexual behavior is bad if it brings pleasure to both parties. This latter is important. If one party does not receive pleasure then disharmony is increased. The soul created in that situation will be less harmonious than would otherwise be the case.

The soul born in rape may carry that disharmony with it for many lives until its persona can bring it back into harmony.

I am not talking here about the long-term effects upon the people, or other beings, indulging in sexual behavior. I am talking about the moment of the soul's birth. That one of the parties may regret the episode, or suffer long-term disharmony, is irrelevant as far as the harmony of the soul is concerned.

The soul simply takes the harmony that it finds at the instant of creation.

There is no birth control for souls. You cannot prevent a soul coming into being if an orgasm occurs.

If a soul is energy, how can it be either harmonious or disharmonious? Why doesn't its energy dissipate? Let's take the dissipation problem first.

All energy is. In the physical world, one form of energy can transform into another—the energy of the sun, for example, is transformed into the energy that allows vegetation to grow, oceans to heat, skin to tan. This might be called dissipation, but it is not. It is merely the transformation from one sort of energy to another. The energy itself never ceases to exist. There will be constant transformations from one form to another—energy to matter, which is itself a form of energy, matter back to energy, the power of a waterfall to electricity, decaying vegetation to nutritious soil or coal, soil to vegetation and coal to heat. Energy itself is an event and, like any other event, has ripples which go on throughout eternity. The energy that is a soul is no different. It is part of the energy of All There Is. Because that energy is universal and constant, so a soul is universal and constant.

The question of disharmony is easier to deal with. All energy changes as it passes through various filters—the rays of the sun are changed as they pass through the filter of the ozone layer, although they are still recognizably the sun's rays. So it is with souls. As they pass from existence to existence they pass through a number of filters, as it were. I will deal with this in more detail later, but for the moment it is sufficient to say that a soul can take on harmony or disharmony from its lives, as it can from its birth.

FIFTEEN — THE HARMONY OF THE SOUL

For one of your kind to be in harmony internally, your minds must be in harmony and you must have a harmonious soul. It is very difficult, but not entirely impossible, for your minds to be harmonious if your soul is not.

As I said before, a soul is born through an act of love. If that act is mutually pleasurable, then the soul will be harmonious at its birth.

But that is not the only thing which can affect a soul. A disharmonious death will affect the soul of the dying being. A death surrounded by love and care will add to the harmony of the soul—and to the harmony of the souls giving the love and providing the care.

A life spent being subject to the disharmony of others will affect the soul, as well as the minds, of one of your kind (since most other creatures are naturally harmonious, this aspect of the creation of disharmony is almost unique to your species). Too much disharmony can lead to the extinction of a soul.

By your acts of selfishness, greed or cruelty, you create disharmony in both minds and souls.

But no soul is so disharmonious that it cannot be brought into harmony by its persona. This is important. If you can make contact with your persona you can be brought into harmony of both mind and soul. And you can!

What does harmony of soul feel like? Why does it matter? Harmony feels like optimism. It is the only word that your kind would understand that I can use. But it is not the particular optimism that you feel, for example, when you think that you will win a horse race or get ahead in your career. No, it is like the optimism of feeling love. In a very real sense, it is feeling love, the love of All There Is.

All There Is is love and this love is there for every being in all universes. Yet only a harmonious soul can feel this love. Without that feeling there is no comfort, without that comfort life is empty, pointless.

Each of you has a persona waiting for you to make the move that will allow it to bring you to that comfort, that love, that harmony. If you will permit me I will, through these words, lead you to make that contact.

SIXTEEN — KNOWING A PERSONA

As I said before, a persona has no physical existence. It is merely a link between yourself and the Universal Consciousness.

All There Is speaks to you all the time through everything, but it is impossible to make sense of what is said without the help of that link. It is rather like trying to listen to a tape speeded up many thousands of times. Someone or something has to be able to slow down the tape to filter the cacophony.

If you need to feel the universal love of All There Is, and you all do, then you need the help of a persona to bring that love to you in whatever form is most suited to you.

Personas can speak to you in many ways. Some, like me, can be channelled, others speak directly to your minds in the form of images or words. Each of you has a persona—every living being has. They have been called, in the past, guardian spirits, auras, spirit guides and so forth. They are the angels that people have made such a fuss about lately!

In a disharmonious world they are rarely contacted. The vast majority of channels, for example, are contacting their own minds rather than a persona. Most spirit guides guide only to the bank accounts of their promoters. Most angels are imaginary.

So, how can you recognize a persona? There are three basic tests that you can use to make sure that you have contacted your persona. First you can ask yourself: Does this contact seem full of love? Secondly: Does this contact encourage doubt, even in its own existence? Thirdly: Does this contact demand anything of you besides love? If the answers to the first two tests are 'yes' and the third 'no,' then you <u>may</u> have made contact with your persona.

You still may be talking to one of your minds, or a group of them. You must live with this cntity for a while, get used to it. Watch it carefully for the slightest tendency to any emotion other than love of yourself and all around you. If it should ever ask for obedience, ignore it immediately. If it ever suggests harm to any other being, cast it out. If it cannot bring you comfort, dismiss it—it is merely part of your own subconscious.

You are now one step nearer to recognizing your persona. But you will want to be sure, not slip into easy belief. One final test is needed. Ask it to take your will! Your own consciousness or subconscious cannot take your own will. You will feel a blank, a nothingness, if you are merely talking to yourself. If you feel a relief, and yet a sense of freedom, then you have probably found your persona. Your persona will not take your free will away, only guide it, with your daily, active, consent, to make it one with that of All There Is.

If that last is what you feel, then you have made contact.

SEVENTEEN — REINCARNATION

ut why make contact with your persona? If you are reasonably happy with life, why go through the process of bothering about this being that links you to All There Is?

I will tell you. You and it may well be together for many lifetimes and it would be prudent to make sure you see eye-to-eye with it.

Many lifetimes? The major religions treat what you call the 'after-life' in, basically, one of two ways: Your soul goes to a heaven as a reward for your goodness (whatever that means) in this life or you are reborn on some cycle of lives until you reach oneness with God. In each case there is the assumption of a test—this life tests you, and you are rewarded for your good deeds.

All of this is absurd. The test is a power-play invented by the promoters of these faiths and intended to keep you in line. There is no test as far as the Universal Consciousness is concerned.

When you die, as you would put it, your soul has the choice of being reborn, or not. There is no hurry for it to choose, time has no meaning for a soul. When it decides to be reborn it has an infinity of choices open to it.

There is no cycle because there is no better or worse form of life. All life is equal in the eyes of All There Is.

Your soul may be reborn in the body of an ant, or an amoeba, or a human or a blade of grass. It will choose the experience it wants. Does it want a long, rather uneventful life? If so it might choose to be a tortoise, a redwood or a lobster. Does it want a short life surrounded by love? A human with a severe handicap might be appealing, if the family seems loving.

Sometimes the disharmony in the soul will drive it to rebirth in a disharmonious situation—it may deliberately choose a dysfunctional family, or be born into a famine or war.

But if you have made contact with your persona and taken the first steps toward harmony within yourself and between yourself and All There Is, your soul will choose a more harmonious life.

Many souls repeat types of lives—dogs may remain dogs, trees perhaps stay trees, viruses may enjoy being viruses, humans might continue being humans. A soul may come back into life many times as a woman, for example, or as a man. The point is that the choice is there.

I will discuss the mechanics of the choice later, but for now I want to say that this rebirthing can be a pleasurable adventure for you and your persona. And I want to emphasize that there is no test.

EIGHTEEN — MORE ON THE FAMILY

It may be thought, from what I have said, that I am against the family. That is not true. The family is vital. What I am against is a family that breeds disharmony amongst its members.

The nuclear family fails for several reasons:

First, it places too much of the burden of child-rearing upon its adult members. More of this later.

Second, it does not provide the range of comfort and experience that a child needs to properly develop.

Third, it perverts the roles of men and women.

And finally, it places an almost intolerable burden on the sexual roles of the adult and child members of the family.

In short it is unnatural. It is as unnatural as a grouping consisting of a man with many concubines or a commune where partners are shared. All of these are aberrations. If you forget everything else that I say, remember this: You cannot have harmony without a harmonious family system.

I have said before that a family, or tribe, should be as large as a village. It should be a cooperative environment, and this cooperation should extend to the business of child rearing. A child should recognize all the women of the family as mother figures and gain experience from each. Likewise all the men of the family should be father figures.

From each, the child takes some clue to adulthood. As important, from the child's point of view, is that he or she can escape the temporary disharmony in one or both parents and find comfort in another part of the tribe.

A child should be loved by all as the hope of the tribe.

The burden of child rearing is thus eased for parents because, in difficult times, there are always those who will be happy to care for another child. And this is good for the child. Without this range of experience, a child will not grow up. I have said this before, but it must be repeated. A child trapped within a nuclear family will never fully grow to emotional maturity. The child will be emotionally and mentally crippled for life, and for the next life, as his or her soul takes the disharmony with it.

NINETEEN — MEN AND WOMEN

Contrary to what some sages of your kind say, there is a difference between men and women, and there are different roles. If this were not so, evolution would not have bothered with two sexes. This is not a matter of equality. Men and women have different emotional ranges and responses, different capabilities.

I realize that this is not a fashionable thing to say. But if one sex tries to emulate the other, they will both tend to disharmony.

Consider men and women. Forget the platitudes of feminism or antifeminism. Consider the truth. Men cannot bear children. The bodies of men and women are different. They have different emotional and hormonal cycles. Look, let me give you an analogy:

An automobile is made up of a body and an engine. Neither is more important than the other, one cannot function adequately without the other. So it is with the sexes.

What are the roles? How are they different?

In what you call primitive societies, the work of supporting the clan is divided between the men and the women thus: The men hunt and construct dwellings, the women gather roots and berries and tend children.

Of course your society is much more complicated, but the biological differences are rooted in the needs of the tribe or clan. Notice I said clan rather than village. Your kind evolved to meet the needs of a hunter-gathering society.

I do not propose that you go back to hunting and gathering! I do propose that you examine the roles the sexes play at work and in the home. Ask, for example, what sort of occupation is a hunter best suited to? What a gatherer? What is the role of a shelter constructor in the home?

I am not going to provide a list of suitable occupations and household roles. I am only saying that if you wish to increase the harmony in your society you must frame the way you operate in that society on the basis of those questions.

I know that it is difficult. You have lost the sense of belonging that a small homogeneous society brings and you are riding the crest of a wave toward your own destruction.

Do not think that I am trying to say that women should remain in the home and not work. Far from it. Nor am I saying that men must carry the entire burden of economic providing. I am saying, perhaps pleading would be a better word, that you must realize your strengths and celebrate your differences!

TWENTY — LOVE AND SEX

Your kind are forever trying to differentiate between love and the desire for sex. The assumption is that somehow love is pure while sexual feelings are not. You allow that the coupling of man and woman is pleasurable, if carried out under the correct circumstances, but is otherwise a lower form of activity.

Let me say that the distinction is unreal. Sex unaccompanied by love has nothing to do with the desire for carnal intercourse. It has everything to do with power, with enslavement and with self-esteem. Or a combination of all of these.

Both love and the desire for sexual fulfillment are universal. Love is what motivates this and all universes, sex is the method by which all living things are created (the self-division of a single cell, while it is a sexless act in itself, is only possible because of the larger context of the body it inhabits, which, of course, is the result of an act of sex).

I have spoken of love before and I have discussed the love of All There Is and of personas. Now I must talk about the love of one human for another. Let me first say that, in harmony, love is the natural feeling of one person for another.

Every feeling of love is a bit of harmony. Of course love that lasts a lifetime contains more harmony and is more beneficial for the soul than love that lasts but a short while. But all love is good of itself—even if it is only one-sided!

A brief encounter that leads to an act of intercourse, provided the act is desired by both parties, can be described, truly, as love. I realize that some of you will not agree. So be it. In the eyes of All There Is that act is one of love and a small bit of harmony is created.

But what if that brief encounter leads to regret? All of the regret you can muster will not erase that harmony.

What of intercourse between father and daughter, mother and son? Surely that is bad!

Why? You have social taboos against what you call incest in your particular society, but other societies have viewed this relationship with more openness. The harm comes from the social stigma, not from the act itself.

Of course, and this is a vital caveat, there must be informed consent on both sides. Sex between a father and his four-year-old daughter is disharmonious—for both. That kind of incest is nothing short of rape and is symptomatic of a deep emotional sickness within the father.

In any act of sex, consent must be informed. The child must be old enough to know what he or she is doing and feel the requisite desire. The age at which a child is able to make this kind of informed consent will vary from society to society, race to race and family (in my sense of the word) to family since developmental patterns vary widely. There is an argument to be made that a girl brought up in a nuclear family may never reach sufficient emotional maturity to make an informed consent. Such a woman, even in adulthood, will suffer what is tantamount to rape every time she submits (from her point of view) to physical intercourse. This is an aspect of sexual relations that your kind often ignores, to your societal peril.

TWENTY-ONE — HUMAN SEXUALITY

Let me say at once that no consensual act of sex is wrong! No, none. The consent must be informed—if one partner had AIDS, for example, and did not tell the other, then the act would be uninformed and thus rape.

Human sexual acts fall into four basic categories:

Intercourse between male and female.

Intercourse between male and male.

Sexual activity between female and female.

Sexual activity with other species.

None of these are wrong of themselves, all can lead to harmonious souls being created. However not all are natural to your species. I have mentioned that you are, essentially, a hunter-gatherer society.

Therefore what is natural, is natural to such a society.

Male/female intercourse is natural because it leads to the continuation of the species. The others require more detailed examination.

Before I begin this somewhat controversial discussion, let me repeat that sex and love are indissolubly linked. Both are necessary. Most acts of sexual activity are also acts of love and sex is one of the engines that drives the self-realization of the Universal Consciousness or All There Is.

Let me also repeat that all acts of sex which result in orgasm give rise to souls and that a harmonious act of sex—one that has love and pleasure on both sides, however brief—will give rise to a harmonious soul.

It is important to bear these facts in mind as we move on. I am not going to discuss moral issues. When I say natural or unnatural I am not talking about morality. I am using the word natural to mean two things: one, that which conforms most to your evolutionary heritage and two, that which is most harmonious.

Morality is only harmony and love. That which leads to the most of each is good in the eyes of All There Is.

I also want to say that, in light of the above, all laws regarding sexual conduct are senseless. More senseless than other laws. I believe we are now ready to move on together.

TWENTY-TWO — HOMOSEXUALITY

irst let me say that the sexual drive in females of your species is stronger than that of males. By and large males have weaker sex drives. This may be bad news to some men!

I have said that you must look to the hunter-gatherer society when trying to work out the best arrangements for your society, and adapt their patterns to suit your more complex lifestyle. This is true of sex as well.

In the original 'primitive' societies—no examples of which now exist—the men, having constructed temporary shelters for the clan (or prepared the caves), would go off hunting, often for days on end. The women would gather roots and berries closer to the shelters and care for the children.

During these times the drive of the men—their energy—was devoted exclusively to the hunt. Their limited sexual drives were sublimated to allow them to focus on the often dangerous job at hand.

The women had no such outlet for their, greater, drive. For this reason the sexual organs of men and women evolved to cope with this situation. A man can only find true satisfaction in intercourse. A woman gets little satisfaction in this way. Hers comes primarily from direct stimulation of her clitoris.

It matters little to a woman, sexually, if this stimulation is carried out by a man or a woman. Women naturally, therefore, turned to each other for their sexual gratification, especially when their men were away or when their men's drives were inadequate. Men, on the other hand, had no need for homosexual gratification as their drives were directed, to a large extent, toward the hunt.

Thus bisexual activity is natural for a woman. She can find satisfaction in both woman-to-woman and woman-to-man activity. It is therefore natural for a woman to be bisexual whereas it is not for a man. Men indulging in homosexual acts are acting against their evolution and this will, over the long term, lead to disharmony. The one caveat to this is in the case of genetic homosexuality among men. It is true that a chromosomal distortion can make a man select another man for his mate and that this distortion can be inherited. However this is not generally the case, and most male homosexuality is the result of nurture.

I must repeat that none of these acts is wrong in the moral sense, and all may create some harmony and all may be the result of love. However to deny a woman this natural gratification does more long-term harm to your society than to deny homosexual activity to males.

TWENTY-THREE — RELATIONS WITH OTHER SPECIES

emember you are no more or less in the eyes of All There Is than is your dog or your cat or the ant that finds a home in your kitchen. All have souls, all are universes unto themselves, all are part of the divine.

Your relationship to other living things should be based on that simple precept.

The question then arises concerning your need to feed off other creatures and plants in order to survive and to use their labor. What should be your relationship to them?

A soul chooses to be a cow knowing that it is the lot of a cow to produce milk. A soul chooses to be a sheep knowing full well that there are such things as lamb chops. You are forgiven by the souls of these species if you need their milk and their flesh to survive.

What is important is that you do not create disharmony by cruelty. You must recognize that there is a cooperative contract between you and other species—you will provide an environment in which they will be content and they will repay you with their labor or their pelts or their very lives.

If you use a cruel trap to catch your p breaking this contract—soon there will be no more animals to trap. The production of veal is disharmonious, as are all ways of raising hens other than free-range.

Similarly your relations with domestic pets should be based on the idea that they are freely with you. By your mutual love you can create harmony that will stand your souls in good stead.

Anything you do with a member of another species must be based on the assumption that there is a contract between you, and that your souls have jointly and freely gone into this contract. The contract has but one clause: By our relationship we will strive to mutually increase each other's harmony and we agree to knowingly do nothing that will cause suffering to each other.

That is the agreement by which all souls are reborn.

It follows from this that you can do anything with another species so long as you and the other animal find it mutually agreeable. Do not try and use your pet or whatever as a slave with no rights but to serve your pleasure. You will soon lose their love and you will only add to your own disharmony.

In fact, you would be treating these species as the leaders of your religions and the makers and administrators of your laws treat you—as part of their own need for power. I do not wish such disharmony upon you.

TWENTY-FOUR — THE BEGINNING AND END OF LIFE

The essence of life is the soul. When the soul enters the body, and decides to remain there, it can be said that life has started. When the soul departs then life has ended.

The entry or departure of the soul is not always co-incidental with the beginning of bodily growth or the cessation of the heart beat (if we are talking about a species with a heart).

This is important to bear in mind because so much disharmony has been caused by pointless arguments concerning the beginning of life and whether abortion is murder. These debates have no validity, none!

Let me state that prior to the birth of any creature many souls may 'try out' the proto-body. Some will dislike the parents and leave, some will find the probable life-course not suited to them and leave. Sometimes no soul desires that life.

If this latter should happen, the fetus will be still-born or aborted. This latter can be by miscarriage or by the conscious act of the parent or parents. The reasons given by the parents for an abortion can be many but the reality is that no soul wishes that body and the desire for abortion is a signal of this. Once a soul has taken up residence within the body, giving it life, then voluntary abortion is impossible. It is not possible for a mother to choose to abort a fetus with a soul.

It is important not to confuse a fetus, which is a marvelous and wondrous piece of nature's mechanics, with a soul-possessed, and thus living, being. The only true test for the existence of a soul within the fetus is the mother's willingness (I mean unforced willingness) to terminate the pregnancy. If she cannot bring herself to abort the fetus then you can be reasonably certain that a soul has permanently taken up residence, so to speak. That mother's wishes to keep and bear the child should be defended at all costs regardless of any questions about the mental and physical state of the resulting child.

At the other end of life, too, appearances can be deceptive. What you call 'vital signs' can continue to be present even after the soul has left the body. This is particularly the case when death is a disharmonious experience. The soul will sometimes be able to escape this disharmony by leaving prior to the cessation of bodily function.

You must not try to force a woman to disharmoniously bring life into existence, or prolong a life artificially, especially if that life will be painful or disharmonious. Keeping a deeply comatose person alive is absurd — the soul has gone.

Medicine, for all its genius, cannot prolong life beyond the span allotted at the start of life. When a soul agrees to enter a body and begin a life, it knows for how long it will be, barring accidents, alive. The job of medicine must be, in the case of a terminal illness, to ease the soul from the body with as much harmony as possible.

I have said it before, and I will reiterate it now: It is vital that a child be born into love and that a person die amidst love. Birth and death are the most important phases of a soul's participation in life.

TWENTY-FIVE — EVOLUTION

Both the Darwinists and the creationists are wrong!

Those propounding the present theories of evolution assume that it proceeds through the survival of the fittest. In this way, so they say, individuals of a species, under pressure from environmental changes, produce some aberration which makes it easier to survive. The genes responsible for this mutation are passed down to that individual's off-spring and so a new species is created more suited to the prevailing conditions. These ones are the fittest and will drive out those without the mutation.

I realize that this is simplistic, but I need to state the theory in its most basic terms so that I can explain its half-truth.

First remember that the earth you live on is a living organism and that it itself regulates the environment for its own benefit. You, and every species of creature on the earth, are part of the earth's environment. Each of you play a role in protecting that environment and keeping it stable.

In other words the earth is a cooperative, not a competitive, place. When a species evolves, it evolves in order to cooperate better. For example, it is absurd to ask who benefits more from the best agriculture: the farmer, the consumer or the corn which is grown.

In reality all three benefit — they are all part of the contract I spoke of before. Growing corn in the most efficient way, so as to produce the most healthy crop, is to the benefit of the corn, just as it is to the farmer and the consumer.

So it is with every stage of evolution. A species evolves because its adaptation will help many many species, indeed the entire planet, not merely itself. This is a very harmonious arrangement—the survival of the fittest to cooperate.

The creationists assume some master plan. A Godhead sits somewhere like an all-powerful bureaucrat with a master plan for each species, on each planet, and plots its course. What rubbish!

The planet survives through a constant process of adaptation, which you label evolution. If there were some immutable master plan there would be no free will, since every action of every individual would be dictated at the start of the universe—indeed at the start of all universes. But there was no start to all universes. All There Is, *is.*

Is it all, then, some accident? No. No more than the corn growing is an accident. But neither is it predetermined, any more than the corn growing is. I will discuss causality later, for the moment remember you live in a constantly changing, basically harmonious, cooperative, environment.

TWENTY-SIX — A BLADE OF GRASS

I once asked a man who had come to talk to me, through my child Bob, what he thought of a blade of grass. This man had come seeking the answers to what your kind believe to be the most fundamental questions of the universe—the nature of God and the reasons for your very existence.

I posed the question. He was nonplussed. He had not come to talk about grass! "I never think of blades of grass!" he said in a state of some indignation. "Then I have nothing to say to you!" I replied. He left saying that I was an evil spirit.

If it is evil to be concerned with every living thing, then I am, indeed, evil. I do not accept the hierarchy that is sometimes seen in your school textbooks—the one showing single-celled creatures at the bottom and mankind at the top. I only accept specialness in the sense that every living thing is special in the eyes of All There Is. There is no gradation of specialness.

But there are gradations of love. Acceptance of the uniqueness and specialness of a blade of grass does not mean that you must love each blade of grass as much as you do your child, or even your dog. To try to do so leads only to disharmony and madness.

I expect you to love All There Is, the universe, your world, your fellow lifeforms, your species, your neighbors, your family and yourself—from the abstract to the intensely particular—in an ascending order of magnitude. This is healthy love. Any other order is disharmonious. You must learn to love yourself above all else—for only then can you truly love anything.

And the blade of grass? What should our man have thought of a blade of grass? He should have thought that there is a wonder in all living things. He should have pondered the question of whether every living thing has a soul, and, if it has, what then is the relationship between a man or a woman and another soul?

And if the blade of grass has a soul, does it then have feelings? If it does, what are those feelings?

And if the blade of grass has feelings, how should we treat it so as to show we recognize its feelings?

And if we wish to explore the way in which it is best to live with a blade of grass, are we then forced into a position of doing nothing because we might hurt the feelings of something?

But he asked none of these questions. There was a God, and there was a Universe and there was Man and he wanted to know the interrelation between them. The Eternal Question!

The answer lies in the questions you ask of a blade of grass and the love you give it as a fellow sentient inhabitant of your world.

TWENTY-SEVEN — MORE GRASS

I like to talk about blades of grass, they are such a lovely symbol. You walk over them every day—treating them as you would the piles of a synthetic carpet. Yet the most profound questions that you can ask are there to be answered in the mere act of looking at an individual blade.

You can see in that blade a soul unadorned with minds, untrammelled by disharmony, totally at one with All There Is. Yet it is dependent on the circumstances around it—its life chances are better in a well-watered lawn than in a dense forest where it has to struggle to find the minimum light necessary to give it the vitamins it needs for sustenance and for the miracle of chlorophyll.

And that answers another Great Question—the relationship of God to Man. God is simply All There Is, the oneness of everything, the consciousness made up of the consciousness of everything—even the consciousness of inanimate things. This God is also interdependent—every part of its consciousness (yes every part!) is dependent on every other part. A butterfly on a planet orbiting a star in a distant galaxy is dependent, to a very real degree, on a butterfly that flapped its wings ten million years ago in a remote corner of your planet.

Since both butterflies are light years apart there is another lesson there—the interconnectedness of time. The blade of grass understands more about time than you do since you are caught up in the span between birth and death.

Look, drop a pebble into the center of the vastest ocean. You can comprehend, perhaps, that the ripples will go on until they wash against the toes of a thousand vacationers on four or five continents.

It is more difficult to realize that the shock-waves of that pebble continue through the continents themselves and have a profound effect on the future of the planet. When? It is a meaningless question since the answer is always—from the moment that the thought arose to the end of eternity.

Each of you is like a pebble dropped into the ocean. Each of you, from the very second of your conception, alters the entire cosmos. Each particle of the Universal Consciousness affects the whole. Each bit of disharmony affects the whole as does each bit of harmony.

And each bit is vital to the whole! Look again at the blade of grass. Each of you is at that moment altering eternity. Your very decision to take the time to look at the blade alters eternity, and if you understand this, you alter eternity for the better.

You see how much a blade of grass has to teach you!

TWENTY-EIGHT — RIPPLES

hen a stone is dropped in the ocean, as we have seen, the ripple effect from that incident goes on forever. Admittedly the shock-waves get weaker with what is loosely called time, but they never die out.

You can understand this phenomenon with the old adage of the frog crossing a road. He hops half the distance with the first jump, half again as much with the second and so on. He never gets to the other side. So it is with the ripples—they never fade completely.

Now I want to say that every action has the same effect. Some of these effects are entirely benign. If you pick and eat an apple (assuming that you are not prone to acidity) the immediate effects are good. The ripples are also benign, even as they go on through the eons of time.

But just as a benign action has an ever-lasting series of consequences, so does a disharmonious one. If you are a holocaust survivor, you will not only carry that trauma on your own soul, but you will pass it on to your genetic offspring and they to theirs for generation after generation.

Look, the cause of your depression might well be an

incident that happened to your great-great-great grandparent. It is as if the incident had been implanted in the genetic make-up of the family. It is like the stone and the ocean—as the ripples spread out they get weaker, but persist.

The failure to recognize this is one of the prime failings of your psychologists. Oh, they go back to the parents, and perhaps to the grand-parents, but to go much further assumes that which they do not wish to assume—that the incident is not traceable by their methods and therefore not curable by their methods. Nor, of course, will it be cured by drugs, shock-therapy, hypnotism or any of the other idiocies that your kind inflicts upon itself.

Strangely enough, your astrophysicists are slowly coming to grips with this phenomenon. They can detect the faint energy created by the 'Big Bang' still rippling through your universe many billions of years after the event.

There is no cessation of anything. The effects of every action last forever. One act of cruelty, for example, will beget effects that will elicit traumas in generations of creatures not yet even evolved.

That is what is meant when I say that disharmony spreads like a contagion. It is important that you measure every action against this eternal effect standard and make sure you do not give your trust to any who do not.

TWENTY-NINE — MORE RIPPLES

But not only psychology neglects this ripple effect, so does medicine and every social science.

Look, it is pointless to treat a Native American with Western drugs and expect him or her to be cured in the way a European would be. His or her genetic history has had only two hundred or so years' experience of drugs and to treat such a person as if they were an Italian or a German or a Scot is an insult to their body and will only cause disharmony.

I am not saying you should withhold all drug treatment, only that it should be administered with thought and with a realization that there may be more effective cures in harmony with the person's genetic inheritance.

My families, being small and without bureaucratic defenses for static ideas or a need to maintain professional casts, will be much more flexible and realize that healing is a cultural and spiritual process as well as a medical one.

Again it is ripples, the generations of shamans have left their mark on all those who carry the Native American genetic code to the Nth degree. The disease may be the same, but the way it attacks the body may be entirely different and its treatment must recognize the difference.

I can heal, in part, because I see the past of each person and their inheritance and I can talk to the body in such a way as to best stimulate its own immune system. I may not always succeed—the mind may resist attempts to cure the body.

Armed with this knowledge you will one day throw off the shackles of your present reliance on drugs and learn to talk to the viruses and bacteria that cause your illnesses. You will learn to reason with them and explain to them that they are better off letting their host survive.

How do you do this? You are not yet ready to even attempt it, there is too much disharmony. But eventually the ripples and the grass will tell you how to do it.

Oh! Ati! Grass again!

Yes, yes, I confess it. Grass again. You did not think I was going to let go of that blade so easily, did you, really? There is a fundamental difference between the diseases that attack a blade of grass and a human being ("Of course!" I hear you shout in derision). But really. Study that difference and you will slowly come to see illness in a different and more helpful light.

I love blades of grass, they tell you so much. Harmony, medicine, the relationship of the universe to Humankind..............!

THIRTY — CONTEXTS

I have said that an event has ripples that last forever, and I want to come back to that later, because there are implications to events that need to be addressed.

For now I want to talk about contexts. I am going to talk about all things, but especially living things. For hundreds of years your kind has looked at all organisms from the standpoint of mechanics. Any organism, from a simple cell to a human being (I am not assuming a hierarchy of importance here, only levels of complexity) has been seen as a sort of biological machine.

You could find out how the machine worked, it was thought, by bringing it into the laboratory and dissecting it, or by observing it in a controlled environment — such as a zoo.

You could even talk about the cell without relating it to the environment in which the cell operates if you knew how the cell functioned mechanistically.

I want to tell you that this whole system of biology is fundamentally wrong!

It is wrong for a very simple reason, which can be

stated starkly thus: A rabbit in the field is not the same animal as a rabbit in the laboratory. A rabbit is only a rabbit in the context in which a rabbit operates. The same goes for a cell, or even an atom. An atom is influenced to a huge degree by its surrounding atoms and nearby molecules. Move the atom and you change it. Replace the cell and you change it.

The context is part of the organism—no, I do not mean the organism is part of the whole, that is a truism which even a biologist would be forced to accept. I mean that the context in which an organism finds itself becomes part, a vital part, of the organism itself.

Oh, I know that the organs of the laboratory rabbit and the wild rabbit are in the same place. But they are not the same organs. They are still within the context of the rabbit, to be sure, but as the rabbit is not the same rabbit, it follows that they are not the same organs. It follows further that to ask how they function under laboratory conditions and extrapolate that to the wild rabbit is a pointless exercise if you are looking for exact parallels.

There is an interaction between the environment and the individual which makes the mechanical model irrelevant. The consequences of this are fundamental, for you must view life differently than you have. You must also view the environment differently—you cannot change the environment without changing yourself, not even in the smallest way! This has implications in every sphere, but more particularly in the disciplines of biology, medicine, psychology and sociology. Think about it.

THIRTY-ONE — ENERGY EVENTS

This is going to be the most radical part of the book. Get ready for it. Here we go.

The universe is merely a series of energy events! All matter can be reduced to these events, and is created by these events. I can show this most easily in the growth of the embryo. The initial event is the coupling of a man and a woman (leave aside test-tube babies, they are an aberration). This event creates matter. The proto-baby does not so much draw upon the mother for its growth, the mother rather provides the context for it. The event takes on a life of its own and matter, in the form of bone, tissue, organs and so forth, is created.

I see a grudging acceptance of this. Let us go on.

Remember this: Every event involves energy. The one cannot be viewed independently of the other, for the event provides the context for the energy. You know that matter can be reduced to energy (look at burning wood in a fire, or electricity). What is not so readily grasped is that the reverse can also happen, but only in the context of the right event.

So with the embryo. The event is the mating, the lovemaking provides the energy, the energy becomes matter within the context of the event.

And that is not a unique case. Matter is being created all the time. There is a cycle of events, with energy creating matter, which in another event is reduced to energy, which then, coupled with another event, becomes matter again. Energy itself is ceaselessly being created—by events! You both use and create energy when you walk just as a turbine both uses and creates energy when it makes electricity. Both the use and the creating are in the context of an event which is the initial decision to walk.

That initial decision used almost no energy in the physical sense yet through it a considerable amount is used and created. The decision is the event context.

Of course the above is a very simplistic way of putting it all and there is a very complicated interaction of events happening all the time which shapes all things. The most important of these is the constant event of the Universal Consciousness. It is this that provides the context within which all things are created.

If your scientists follow this line of discovery then they will find not just the prime cause of the universe—the initial event—but also something far more exciting: *God!*

THIRTY-TWO — SICKNESS

What is illness? What is the relationship between disease and mental health?

I want to begin by stating the obvious: Some illnesses have a physical cause unrelated to the mental condition of the patient. The Black Death, Cholera, Yellow Fever, Typhoid—these are just some of the diseases which are spread by living organisms that have found a receptive home in an unfortunate individual. These microorganisms are, of course the main predators facing mankind—the others having been effectively defeated long ago. The best way to treat such diseases is by a combination of medical care and mental therapy with a skilled practitioner and/or spiritual practice (For more on this see my monograph Healing).

I am not against physicians, not at all. They are not my enemies, nor yours. They are, however, insufficiently trained and are locked into a system that permits them little time to come to the truth about disease.

The extent to which a human being will become ill depends on his or her immune system, the home guard, if you like. There are two immune systems operating within you: The physical immune system, which guards against disease and attacks potentially dangerous viruses and bacteria, and the mental immune system.

This second guards against your taking on the disharmony of another. A good psychologist or therapist will have been trained to use this to 'distance' him or herself from the patient. A harmonious person does not need this training. However if one of your kind already has a tendency to self-hate or depression then they will catch these from another with similar tendencies. It is rather like a radio signal being sent out from one brain and being received by another.

I want you to bear this in mind as we discuss illness a bit further because it has some important implications for medical practice.

In many cases a disease may have no obvious physical causes, and yet the patient is quite ill from symptoms which closely mimic a known condition. The real cause of the illness in this case lies within the mind(s) of the individual. A person suffering from guilt, self-hate or depression is constantly telling his or her body that they are no good. In some this will lead to disfigurement through over-eating or anorexia. In others the body responds to more specific orders from the mind(s).

Look at it this way: A mind is a very obvious thing, the complexity and the subtlety of the consciousness come from the interaction of a number of minds. Because a mind is simple the instructions it gives to the body are simple and obvious. A person feeling under great stress will often say that he or she is carrying a great burden and will feel it quite literally in stiff shoulders. A man or woman not wanting to go to work to face a trying situation will complain of leg cramp.

THIRTY-THREE — SICKNESS TWO

Now, what happens if the minds of an individual are so disharmonious that they want to kill that person? Frequently the method of choice is not a bullet, or a noose or a pill but a disease.

One or more errant minds within the individual has decided that he or she has no right to live or, in punishment for some supposed crime, must be made subject to pain. The mind is aware of the effects and symptoms of, say, cancer or lupus or Parkinson's or multiple sclerosis. Signals are sent out from the brain to the body that the body has the disease.

Often, as for example in the case of lupus or arthritis, the body will be instructed that a viral enemy is in the joints. The immune system rushes to attack that area. Of course no virus is found, but the brain continues to send out the signals. The sheer number of cells of the immune system within the area of the joint cause the victim swelling and excruciating pain. The physician treating the patient will often prescribe powerful anti-inflammatory drugs, which will do further harm through their side-effects.

Just in the same way the immune system itself can be used by the mind(s) to attack all the organs of the body, ultimately destroying it.

The symptoms must be seen as messages from the mind(s) and must be read as such. Remember, however, that a mind is simple and that the messages are obvious and meant to be so.

Just as the cause of these illnesses is often mental or spiritual, so, in these cases, must be the ultimate cure. Why, for example, does the patient so hate him or her self? Or, if there is guilt, what is the origin of it? Find the right questions and their answers and the illness will disappear, sometimes quite suddenly and dramatically.

This kind of cure is, of course, the secret behind the miracle cures of Lourdes, or the cures effected by shamans and witch doctors. In essence the patient believes he or she has been freed from the guilt that led to the illness.

The danger that I mentioned of an unprotected mind taking on the self-hate from another individual is real. Sometimes it is taken on with such force that the person receiving the message will feel sympathy pains, will suffer similar symptoms to those afflicting the original person. This is a sure sign that the disease that the person giving out the signals has is mental rather than physical in origin.

This also explains such phenomena as phantom pregnancies. What is not often realized is that a phantom pregnancy does not necessarily reflect a desire on the part of the victim to become pregnant. It can, in fact, signal something quite different. For example it may be that the 'pregnant' person has caught this set of symptoms from another person who is deeply conflicted about their own, real, pregnancy. Or it may be one of your minds trying to punish your body and using the nausea and other side-effects of pregnancy to do so.

I am aware that the above is a very simplistic view of the subject. You will have to forgive me, but I believe I have made the essential point.

There is only one thing that I would like to add, for now, and that is this: The curability of any serious illness depends on one vital ingredient—the patient's genetic make-up. Every individual is genetically programmed to die at a certain age and once that age is reached no amount of medical or psychological or even spiritual treatment will be to any avail. Even if the symptoms of one ailment are 'cured,' another problem will quickly arise and complete the program.

It is most inharmonious to try to preserve the life of an individual whose time has come, it is the work of a healer to prepare that individual for the most harmonious death possible.

THIRTY-FOUR — REALITY

I want to examine a pernicious doctrine that some may say has been validated by what I have just said, and quickly dispose of it. This doctrine is all the more dangerous because it contains a grain of truth amongst its sand of deceit.

It is the doctrine that says that you create your own reality.

Let me first give you the grain of truth that it contains in two parts.

First, everything in the universe is, to some extent, altered by your perception of it. Some of your scientists accept this and it is true.

Second, your destiny is, to some extent, dependent on your will, your energy. Again, this is true.

The key point in both statements, however, is the phrase 'to some extent.'

When these two semi-truths are united into a doctrine that says that because you influence 'reality' through perception you are creating reality, and because you can alter your future through the power of your will you can make the future that you will a reality, a fallacy is created.

The fallacy is clearly shown thus: If you alter by perception, so does every other sentient being in the universe! The amount by which reality is altered by your perception is, therefore, somewhat small. Again, your will is a factor in change and development, but it is only one will among many. The future is, perhaps, like a lottery of competing wills. Your will has to be in the game but is not guaranteed a particular outcome!

But why is the doctrine that you create your own reality so damaging? Because it leads to guilt and disharmony and separates you from the rest of your kind and from everything around you. If you can create your own reality, why are you sick? Disharmonious? Poor? In prison? Surely, under this doctrine, there must be something wrong with your will, you did not will wellness enough, or will sufficient food for your children, or a mortgage or a fine day and so on. Are you not therefore guilty?

It is true that if you have a strong will you can influence events to a greater extent than someone who has a weak will. A person with a strong will to live will live longer, that is obvious. But it is also abundantly true that a strong will is not always a guarantee of success.

So let us hear no more of the doctrine that says that you 'make your own reality.' You do not, in the sense inferred by the doctrine, and that is the end of it.

THIRTY-FIVE — FREE WILL

There is an ageless debate among your species as to whether there is such a thing as free will. Is everything predetermined by God according to a universal plan, or do human beings have the ability to influence their destiny?

Those who rely on psychics, economic determinists and fundamentalist Christians fall into the 'God determines everything' camp—whether their God is a divine presence or whether it is the Marxist view of history.

I take the divine argument more seriously than the Marxist one, since it has an element of logic to it. The argument runs like this: God is omnipresent and omnipotent (both by definition). If He is omnipotent then nothing must be beyond His control. If nothing is beyond His control then it follows that human actions and therefore individual destiny must also be controlled by Him. It's neat, but it's false.

The fallacy lies in the definition of God. I do not like the word 'God' because it seems to assume the meaning given to it by Christians (and others) which includes both omnipresence and omnipotence and also a separation from the individual. I would use the term Universal Consciousness or All There Is. By doing so I can craft a definition which happens to be true.

I have said before that the Universal Consciousness is omnipresent. Everything that exists is part of it. I have also said, when talking of minds, that this Consciousness is in a constant state of self-creation and self-realization.

The effect of this is that, as far as predestination is concerned, the future does not exist and therefore is not, in any way, determined. The Universal Consciousness is therefore a creative force, but not omnipotent.

The future, then, is created by a process of self-realization by the Universal Consciousness or All There Is. But you are a part of All There Is, you are a part of that self-realization. It is as if you and the entirety of all the existing universes without number were on this journey together. Your actions help shape the future and have an influence upon it.

It follows from this process of self-realization that there can be no master plan. If there is no master plan that determines the future, then the possibility of free will emerges.

Free will, however, does not mean that the omnipotence once reserved for God has been transferred to you. Free will has limitations, you can only exercise it within narrow confines, some of which—economic, societal, psychological—are imposed upon you by your society. Many of these limitations are needless and are, in fact, greatly disharmonious. We will discuss them later.

THIRTY-SIX — THE FUTURE

I am sorry, but you cannot know the future. Nor can psychics, seers, politicians or economists. The future, as I said when discussing free will, does not exist.

What then does it mean when I say that I can see all possible futures, if none of them exist? Let me explain it this way: The future is made up of an infinite number of strands, a chaos of causes. You clap your hands together, the shock waves from that clap disturb the air around you. The disturbance in the air affects the mating of a pair of butterflies. The lack of mating means that fewer butterfly larvae will be born. This means that more vegetation will survive intact and so on and so on and so on. The events that form the future have their origins in a multiplicity of random causes, some as simple as the clapping of hands or the falling of a branch from a tree or a spider's catching (or not catching) its prey.

This makes the future unseeable to any human. There is an almost infinite number of possible futures, an almost infinite number of possibilities. I say almost because there is a limit to the number of events that occur, and since each event is a cause, with other events, of future events, there is a finite, though tremendously large, number of possible futures.

The paradox is that the further you look into these possible futures the clearer becomes the perception of the future. However human minds are not equipped to perform this task. Let us say that you have, at any moment, a trillion possible futures. By definition the future starts now. Really, at this moment you have over a trillion possible futures. Only one will come to pass—your next moment. Then you have a trillion possible futures again.

Since you have free will you can eliminate billions of these trillions of possibilities. By remaining in your seat reading this book you have eliminated many millions. To a large extent your own will can determine your future. Your will is one factor in the future of every other particle of existence.

Now I, as a persona, can see all of these strands as events cause other events and wills shape their course. I can see the likely outcomes though I cannot always give you precise times. To some extent my own perception is one of the determining factors in any given outcome. In some cases my sense of a likely outcome is so strong that I can feel certain enough to make a prediction.

But, as with the Universal Consciousness, the ability to predict the future is not to determine it and the preference for one future over another is not to order it. The proper development of minds, human or otherwise, is to get to a place where they are able to control what they properly can and adjust to what they cannot. The future is yours to influence and to speculate about. Remember that all your actions contribute to the future of all the other members of your species and your planet and act accordingly.

PART TWO: THE WAY TO HARMONY

COME TO ME

Come to me, my arms are waiting.
Sink deeply into my presence.
Leave your body there, you have no need of it.
Leave your minds, they will not follow you.
Sink into me, sink into me.
You are drifting through darkness.
It is not the darkness of despair
It is not the darkness of loneliness.
All around you there is love,
The darkness is like a cocoon, enveloping you.

In that darkness your eyes open.
They are not the eyes of your body
They are the eyes of your soul.
Look into eternity with me
It is pulsing with energy and with love.

Rest. Allow yourself peace.
You are where no harm can come.
You are safe, held, cherished, loved.

Hear my words now, and no other.
Let me hold you and love you.

You are drifting through the eternal universe.
You are timeless and without care.
This is my realm and I am your guide.
Give me your trust as a small child would its parent
And I will hold the child within you.

Drift in my arms. Your soul in my arms.
Allow yourself to wonder at your own peace
And accept it. And accept it. And accept it.
Accept that you are my child.
Accept that you have my peace.

This is love. Not the love of man and woman.
Not the love of possessions, or power.
This is the love of total harmony for itself.
This is the love you now share,
This is the harmony you now feel.

You are like a feather, beautiful, complex—
Floating on the cool breeze of an early summer day.
You feel the light eternity of the soul.
You trust the breeze to carry you on its will.
I am the breeze and I will you love.

The wind in your ear calls:

I am the earth
I am the sky
I am All There Is.

TWO — CONTACTING YOUR PERSONA

I have said before that every living organism has a persona. Virtually all living creatures have no need to contact their persona because they already are in contact with it.

It would be absurd to ask whether a tree is in contact—trees have never been out of contact. The same is true of horses or fish or flies. In fact, on your planet, it is only humankind that has lost the innate ability to be at one with the link between a man or woman and All There Is.

But anyone can re-establish that link.

There are, if you like, three stages to the process. The first, and most basic, is that you must need and want that link. You must need and want to be in contact with the Universal Consciousness. There must be in you the feeling that you are alone, cut off from something yet not knowing quite what. If you ache for comfort and support, you are ready.

Next you must overcome the feeling that you must agree with the cynicism of others of your kind and, more important, the cynicism implanted in you by your own mind(s). This is not easy and it is not a question of meditation or the refusal to listen to the doubts of others. It is a matter of giving in to your need, wholly. Nothing else matters except your need to be at one with something beyond yourself.

The third stage is the most difficult of all. Love yourself. Forgive yourself for everything. Cast out self-hatred for you are innocent. Yes innocent! All of you! Whatever you have done you have done because of the intolerable pressures of society based on the twin stupidities of false religions and the nuclear family.

Your families were, for the most part, dysfunctional. How could they not be? The guilt arising from such living conditions is natural. Actions designed to hurt others are a product of that guilt, nothing more. The failure to save your family from drug or alcohol or physical abuse is not your failure. You could not succeed, and you cannot fail at that which is impossible.

You are innocent. Love yourself.

When these three basics are in place—the need, the open mind and the love of self—you are ready for one such as me to lead you to the Universal Consciousness.

THREE — NEED

Each of you is part of the divine, part of the Universal Consciousness, part of All There Is.

But so is the chair you sit on to read these words. Each of you has an eternal soul which will, upon your death, return to the love of All There Is.

But so has your cat and the cold virus within you.

Each of you feels the need to be other than alone in the universe, to be a part of something other than yourselves.

In this last you are unique.

Your cat is secure in the love of All There Is and does not question its place in the Universal Consciousness. The virus has no mind and so cannot even pose the question. Your kind alone, on your planet, feels the need.

It is not the need for blind faith. That is fragile and can be lost at any moment, or transferred to another, equally blind faith.

Sometimes it is no more than an irritant, a feeling that something is missing, the emotional inability to accept that what you see is the sum total of everything. The need is there.

But the coldness of a man on a cross, or the God who issues laws to be obeyed upon pain of eternal damnation, or the God of the conqueror who commands holy war, or the plethora of gods ending in the absurdity of a god for everything, will not truly satisfy that need.

The need is to sink into your God. To be one with your God in the most total sense, to feel your God all around you— every day, every moment, in every action. Yet gods do not fulfil this function. They are answers to questions which beg more questions. They are inventions.

The need to be that intimate with God is really the need to be God! To be divine! And you are.

Give in to that need, recognize your own divinity. Do not be afraid of madness, I am not asking you to think of yourself as a god. I am asking you to recognize your need to be at one with All There Is, to accept that comfort, to answer that need.

FOUR — DOUBT

I welcome doubt. Never be afraid of doubt. Doubt me, doubt All There Is.

But doubt all your preconceptions as well.

Doubt the confining education, doubt the dysfunctional nuclear family, doubt the demanding religions, doubt the wisdom of your leaders, doubt the words written in pompous editorials.

Doubt is the path to All There Is. It is a necessary prerequisite, it is the womb from which will come the sense of oneness with All There Is.

All There Is does not demand faith—how can everything ask for faith? The Universal Consciousness does not demand anything of you. Not faith, not obedience, nothing.

Of course it is uncomfortable to doubt all things, your minds search for eternal verities to help you make sense of the chaos of your world. To have one thing stand still in an ever changing matrix and to fix on that and say, with some relief, 'This I believe and will not doubt!' is, temporarily at least, comforting.

But belief is like a blanket that you pull over you to

hide beneath. It is a blanket provided for you by others of your kind who wish to take you into their own power structure. You are using it to hide from All There Is.

Humankind has the capacity to believe the most absurd things. You have believed in a flat earth, in devils, in fairies, in the ravings of Hitler and the idiocy of the cargo cult of New Guinea and the South Sea Islands—the belief that cargo planes were gods bringing goods for the believers, goods that the white men were keeping from them. Belief is always false. When you say 'I believe,' you are wrong.

The reason that doubt leads you to All There Is, is that it <u>is</u> all there is. Once you sink into that, doubt will not vanish, but each action of doubt will lead you back to the same point, to the same love, to the same comfort. In a sense doubt then becomes irrelevant, you do not need to suppress it.

Doubt is the pathway to being at one with All There Is. Of course, doubt, too, is a part of All There Is, a part of the divine.

I do not need faith, I do not want it. I want only to bring you to love. You will fight that coming, and you will doubt every step of the way.

FIVE — LOVE OF SELF

One of the paradoxes of your kind is that the most self-centered are also the most self-hating. It is as if these people justify their own loathing of themselves by making others dislike them.

These people are a product of a society that pays no attention to the real needs of its young. Since their needs have not been met they find it impossible to recognize the needs of others. This flows on from generation to generation.

Yet few people genuinely love themselves. The body is wrong, the abilities are not right, the hair is the wrong color, they cannot get the right job and so on through the endless whips with which your kind lash yourselves.

And guilt! Guilt over family first and foremost. The sharpest lash of all.

But what if that guilt could be lifted, if you could be found innocent in the court of your own minds? If you could accept your body, know it as perfect? Accept your childhood innocence, all children are innocent. Accept your fallibility, the hardest of all.

Say with me: 'I am innocent.' At first it is difficult. There is a resistance. Your minds say that you are not. All the whips come out and the cuts are deep. Every real and surmised transgression floods into your consciousness.

Say with me: 'I am a part of All There Is, and I am innocent.'

You may feel silly with these words on your lips. They are unfamiliar, unreal. You may not even accept the existence of All There Is. Good.

Say with me: 'I am innocent. I am innocent. I am innocent.' Now let your minds go blank. Picture your own persona—in whatever form you choose—holding you as if you were a baby. You are a baby. Hear your persona say 'I love you, you are innocent, you are perfect.'

Naturally you will awake from this reverie and say that there is no persona and the whips will be out again. It will take many times and must be done every day. Get used to the words: 'I love you, you are innocent, you are perfect.' Hear them often in your minds.

The love of self will flow naturally from this. Do not feel guilt if it takes time, forgive yourself even for that. Everything around you will support you in this journey to self- acceptance and self-love. And you will gain it, and you will contact your persona, and you will meld into the love of All There Is. You will come home.

SIX — INNOCENCE

You are all innocent. In a sense even Adolph Hitler was innocent. To ascribe guilt to him you must also ascribe guilt to his family, to society, to those who followed him, to the nation he led and to the leaders of the other nations who acquiesced in his crimes by their inaction.

But he murdered millions of human beings!

Yes. Each human is a soul and minds. In the eyes of All There Is there is no difference between one soul and another. The soul of your mother or father, your departed loved one or someone you once admired may now be the soul of an ant. Perhaps a carpenter ant, one of the millions that are eating away at your home. You will declare those ants to be vermin, call in an exterminator and have them killed, by poisonous gas!

Hitler did no more. Yet his soul grew so heavy with these acts that it chose not to go on. His soul is dead. In the eyes of the Universal Consciousness that is a tragedy. All life is sacred, part of the divine. But life is transitory.

Of course you regard other members of your kind as supremely important, you even differentiate between races—classing the white or the black or the yellow as more important. You regard the death of, say, a white hostage in Lebanon as more significant that the death of a trainload of brown humans in India.

In the eyes of All There Is that is absurd. But it is also absurd to regard the soul of a human as more important than the soul of an ant or the life of one as more important than the life of the other.

In the eyes of All There Is, a butcher in a slaughterhouse is the same, morally, as a KGB or SS butcher. Yet even these beings are innocent. Even they can find their persona and be led to the love of All There Is. What you have done is unimportant in that respect.

That does not make every act right! There is one crime and one crime only—creating disharmony. Internally among minds, and externally between a being and the Universal Consciousness. That which leads to harmony is good in the eyes of All There Is, that which brings disharmony is bad. That is the only morality.

All souls are innocent in the eyes of All There Is. That is the most important message I can bring to you. The essence of you is your soul, your soul is innocent. Your soul longs for that harmony which is oneness with All There Is, whether it is between lives or during what you call life.

You are innocent. Whatever you have done you can forgive yourself.

SEVEN — THE FIRST STEP TOWARD HARMONY

I will be your guide. I will give you my love and the love of All There Is.

For all those who cannot yet find their own persona, I shall be there for you. I shall hold your minds and comfort you. Come to me.

You feel desperate at times, you feel that the world around you will not accept you. You feel that you cannot cope with your society and you are not one with the universe.

But you can be one with the universe, and the probability is that it is your society rather than yourself that is out of harmony. I will guide you through this nightmare of conflicting emotions and bring you to rest at peace.

You are the child of All There Is. Remember that.

Let your minds just go. Do not be afraid. Just let them go. You will feel a sensation of falling, it will feel that there is no bottom to this fall and yet you are drifting rather than plunging down.

Now you feel that you are caught by loving arms and held. It is as if you were once again a baby. Like an infant you can surrender to the safety of this embrace. It is dark but not frightening, the safety you feel will not let you experience fear.

You can feel my hand on your head, as if stroking your hair—the light, new, hair of a baby. Put down the words and feel it.

Now let me say that you are innocent and that you are loved. You are deep within my consciousness, within me; you can hear the words and they do not frighten you. Give yourself totally to me, in doing so you are giving yourself to All There Is.

I can give you nothing but this safety, this love, this sense of oneness. It is yours to take, all you have to do is accept. There is nothing you can give in return, do not try. I am pleased that you are with me and I treasure your minds as I treasure your soul.

Be calm. You need not come out of this place within me until you are ready. When you feel that readiness you will feel as if a cocoon is around you, protecting you from the disharmony outside. It is important for you to know that you can come back to this place whenever you like. Lie down and let yourself go, drift, let yourself be the child of All There Is. Nothing else is important.

I bring you love. I bring you peace.

EIGHT — DISHARMONY

Come to me. Let your consciousness melt into me. Now, from that place of safety, look out at the world.

Look at the children abused by their parents, themselves trapped in the nuclear family. Look at the terror of the homeless whom no one will claim. Look at the old, shunted into retirement homes and left to rot because their children cannot give them love.

Look at the way animals are treated. Feel the fear of the lobster, its claws bound together. Feel its sense of bewilderment. Look at veal calves made to stand all their short lives in tiny cages without ever having the chance to run or know the outside.

Look at the addiction of your own kind to drugs or alcohol or abuse as they flee from responsibility. Look at the sick abandoned to die alone in hospital wards, surrounded by antiseptic blankness and disharmony.

Look at the starving people and animals in lands made waste by war and futile farming methods that run counter to nature.

These are but small samples of the causes of

disharmony within your species. Is it any wonder that I say that those you class as insane because they cannot function in your society are, in all probability, saner than those who can?

Only the love of All There Is can restore harmony, and only that love can help you. I tell you that it doesn't take prayers or offerings or sacrifices. None of these are of any use.

Priests and clergy are of no use. Environmentalists are of no use. Politicians are of no use. Scientists are of no use. Harmony can only come through you and others coming to be at one with All There Is.

But you can be! Here, within the safety of my embrace you can see the stupidity of your kind and know peace.

But you ask: What must I do? The answer is: Just be! For now, just be. There will be things to do, there will be changes you can make, in small ways at first, in your society and in yourselves. But for now the urge to do is counter-productive. You are not ready.

For now realize the fallacy of most of the doctrines of your kind's leaders and rid yourself of their power. It is they, not you, who are adding to disharmony. Within the safety of myself you cannot cause disharmony. Just be.

NINE — CONTINUATION

It is not enough just to read the words I have written in the last two sections once and move on. Oh I know, your kind likes to get to the last page to see how it ends, but this book is a continuation—so you can resist the temptation!

You must read and re-read what I have said since the beginning of this section. Repeat it aloud. Have it read to you, it is better in any case to travel in company. Follow what I am saying. Allow yourself the luxury of peace. In the words are the keys to the first step.

You must <u>feel</u> that safety if it is to help you. It is insufficient for your minds to have scanned the text. Your whole body must be ready to come to that place which is waiting for you. You must leave your consciousness behind as a separate entity.

Lie there with my words around you. When you know them you will hear them in the sheets of your bed, in the pillow, in the dresser. These are all part of All There Is. These are all part of your support.

Now close your eyes. Do not be afraid of the dark, you are not alone. You are held.

This is not meditation. Meditation fixes on one thing and uses the conscious self to somehow escape, it is a denial of the reality of emotions. That is not what I want. I do not want you to deny emotion—the strongest of them is love and I want you to lose yourself in love. Let your minds go, do not concentrate. The words, the feeling of peace, will come.

You will feel a slight warmth from everything around you. Everything, living or inanimate, has energy and that energy comes from All There Is. Allow yourself to feel it.

I tell you that that warmth is love. Oh, I see you laugh at the idea of getting love from your bedside table! Or from the pillow beneath your head. You are so keen to deny yourself that love that you refuse to acknowledge it unless it comes with the most obvious signs of affection.

You accept it, sometimes, from your dog when he licks your face, or from your child when he eats your food. But you will not allow it as the background energy you have around you all the time. Yet that is a manifestation of the love of All There Is!

You may well do these exercises many times. You must learn to just be. You must learn to accept love. You must learn that you do not have to earn it, it is there all about you.

Maybe you will come to me in that way every day. You will sink into my embrace and let me lead you to the warmth of oneness with All There Is. Maybe only sometimes. I will be there for you.

TEN — JUST BE

It seems hard to 'just be.' I tell you that you cannot find harmony either within yourself or between your consciousness and All There Is unless you can accept the admonition to just be.

What does it mean, 'just be?'

Does it mean sitting around doing nothing? No.

Does it mean spending hours in meditation? No.

Does it mean trying actively to contact your persona? No.

Nor does it mean 'just be yourself,' or 'just be open' or even 'just be alive.'

First, it means recognizing that your very existence is a vital part of All There Is, seeing that you are a part of All There Is.

Second, it means not striving to become in harmony. The more you strive and try the more you will fail. You will create in your consciousness an ideal of what you think you ought to be. You will not be able to live up to this ideal, you will become frustrated and disharmonious. The very thing you wish to achieve will be your downfall!

Thirdly it means acceptance of yourself and your

own perfection. I see the disbelief in your minds at this comment. Perfection? Yes! As you are innocent, so are you perfect!

When you have learned the secret of being able to 'just be' then everything that you do will have the confidence of attainment. You will not fail because you will not try for impossible ideals. You will realize the foolishness of such striving. You will not fail in what you try for because you have a solid base from which to try.

And if you do not always immediately achieve what you aim for, you will not blame yourself or retreat into self-doubt and guilt. Thus striving will not result in your own disharmony.

Now that you see what 'just be' means you will ask what you can do to get into this state. The very question shows that you are not yet there. There is nothing to do, the state of just being is waiting for you. There is nothing to do except to surrender to the comfort and assurance of All There Is.

Your goals, ambitions, desires may all be worthwhile and I would not, for a moment, suggest that you give them up or cease to lead an active life. What I say is that once you have followed the command to 'just be' you will feel the ability to choose the worthwhile from the merely transitory, the possible from the illusory and the harmonious from the disharmonious.

ELEVEN — PERFECTION

In its own way every living creature, from the single-celled amoeba to a human being, is perfect.

You cannot make yourself perfect, you cannot strive for perfection and only your own disharmony can prevent you from seeing your own perfection.

Let me be clear about this, and unequivocal: You are perfect. There are two yous—the you that dwells in the disharmony of the world and that sees only your own failings and the misery of others impinging upon you, and the you that lives as one with All There Is. In a sense, to merge with the Universal Consciousness is to merge these two facets of yourself.

Think about that for a while. The second you already exists.

But what, then, is perfection? Surely one of your kind who thinks of him or herself as perfect would be impossible to live with and would be dictatorial, convinced always of his or her own rightness?

Yes, if you wish to define perfection in human terms. Humans see perfection in terms of what they do, what they believe, what they have, what they desire. All of these are meaningless in the eyes of All There Is. You are not perfect for what you do, or doing would make you perfect! You cannot be perfect for what you believe, when you believe you are wrong! Having cannot induce perfection or the richest would be the best! Desires are merely transitory and perfection is eternal!

Perfection, I repeat, is in being! Being is allowing yourself to feel the oneness and love of All There Is.

So why merge the two yous? Why not just simply discard the first you? Because you would then be less than human! You cannot be perfect and at the same time discard your humanity. You cannot cease to live in the world, or cease to confront the disharmony of others. But when you have recognized, and accepted, your perfect self you will be able to cope with the disharmony around you.

Let me put it this way: I ask you to just be. That state will automatically lead you to recognize your own perfection in the eyes of All There Is. You will feel yourself as one with All There Is. Your disharmony will go.

It is not a simple process since your societies breed disharmony and see perfection in ways that are absurd. You have been taught to strive in ways that are themselves breeders of disharmony. But the first step in the revolution is to recognize that you are perfect and you can gain the peace and comfort of oneness with All There Is.

TWELVE — THE COCOON

You are in a space that is me. If you have been with me as we talked over the last few pages then you are in my space.

There is calm all around you, and peace, in this space. It seems dark, like the black of the universe around you would be if the moon and the stars were to vanish from the night sky. And yet you know that you are not alone.

I am all around you. I am shielding you from every disharmonious thought your minds can throw at you. It is as if you are a baby in a perfect womb, and you are. You are weightless, as if your body does not exist. You are guilt-free. You have no past and there are no considerations of the future to perplex you.

You feel afraid to go out into your world, it is too comfortable in this womb that I have created for you. There is a panic in your consciousness that says that I will suddenly break the spell and you will be left unprotected.

I will not. This cocoon will be around you for as long as you wish. Not in the sense that you will always be in the space that is me. Not in the sense that you feel that you are a baby. Not always in the safety of the womb.

The cocoon will be around you lightly, there to protect you, a place that you can retreat to if you wish.

But now, here, in this space, feel the love I have to give you. It is the love of All There Is, and it is for you always.

There are doubters amongst you who say this is too simplistic, there must be more to peace, more that you have to do to find it, more that you have to prove, even to yourself. No. It is always there for you and I will be there to bring it.

Now feel your own perfection. You are held and you are safe, just feel that you are also perfect. I repeat, you are safe. Put down the words and think, 'I am safe. I am loved and I am safe and I am perfect.'

You are part of the divine, you are part of perfection, you are at one with All There Is. You are at one with yourself. You are perfect.

Feel your consciousness expand to take in that love all around you. It is as if your head was opening up, allowing you to encompass everything. Do not try to feel anything, let the feelings come to you, as love comes to a baby. Be loved for what you are—part of the very fabric of All There Is.

When you leave this space I will still be with you. The cocoon is ready to take you back. The space within me is there for you.

THIRTEEN — STEP TWO

Now that you have seen, from the comfort of your cocoon, the disharmony of the world outside and recognized your own perfection and your innocence in the eyes of All There Is, it is time to take you on the next step toward harmony.

It is primarily internal harmony that I will be dealing with. Remember that you have seven minds and that in order for you to be in harmony, all those minds must work together. There are two ways in which your minds can get out of kilter.

First, there is the case where one or more is seriously damaged by past life experiences or by traumas earlier in this life.

Second, there is the problem, common to your species, where the very fact of living in a dysfunctional family has caused a general sense of depression to be cast over all of your consciousness.

Let me deal with the first situation. Here you have a mind which simply cannot exist with the rest of your consciousness. It might result in retardation because the thinking process is interrupted or it might lead to the desire to physically hurt yourself or even to suicide.

It is impossible to love yourself if one of your minds resolutely refuses to. You must understand that this mind does not want to be there. It is possible that a past life experience so damaged this mind that it did not want re-birth. Life, for it, has been too painful previously. It wants to return to the comfort and peace of the between-life state. It sees two choices. It can shut down completely, or it can try to drive the consciousness it is a part of to death.

But there is hope here. Remember that what that mind is striving for is to be one with All There Is in the only way it knows. That is the key.

It is most likely that mind is still living a trauma that happened to you earlier in this life. I have talked about this aspect of disharmony previously.

The first step toward healing the pain of that mind is to show it love. It may be hard to love what you see as your own desire for suicide, or the backwardness in one you know and care for. Love the mind even though it causes you pain!

Give your love to it consciously. In doing so you will separate you from your feeling of hopelessness. It is not easy. It is not easy to say to yourself that there is something in you, something alien to your natural harmony, that is causing these deep depressions. It is much easier to say that there is a fault in you that some outside expert can cure, or that you can give in to. I will help you love that mind.

FOURTEEN — THE ERRANT MIND

I want to speak in a bit more detail about what I call the errant mind—the one that feels it does not belong in the consciousness. I fear what I am about to say may be a bit abstruse, but I want you to understand fully the journey I am taking you on.

To think effectively a human being needs all of his or her minds to work in some sort of unison—it does not take perfect unison. Thought is the interaction of minds. This interaction may be prevented from being fully effective for several reasons in a normal person.

First, bear in mind the analogy of a computer where the effectiveness of the whole depends on the ability of the operator, the memory, the circuits, the current fed into it, the language used and, finally, the program.

The operator communicates with the program and the program with the hardware by means of electrical impulses. (I realize I am being simplistic and I shall be chided by those of you who understand computers, but bear with me for I am a simple being.)

The minds use similar electrical impulses within the brain to communicate with each other. This takes nanoseconds. If there were a fault with either the program or with the hardware the computer would not be effective. So it is with the consciousness. The consciousness is, if you like, the program and the minds are its constituent parts. If any one mind is ineffective, the whole mechanism breaks down to some extent. The operator is, of course, the soul.

(In passing I would like to say that it amuses me to note that your psychiatrists know very little about how the brain works and your neurologists know little about why. Neither understand the role of the consciousness, which is why people spend years in psychiatric hospitals or have their brains hacked to pieces by neurosurgeons.)

An errant mind, as I have said, can act to try to destroy the human who is afflicted with it or it can simply refuse to function. No amount of conventional therapy will help with the second problem. The first, a suicidal depression, may be alleviated with drugs temporarily at the risk of great harm. The prescribers of these drugs do not understand why or how they work. At the risk of being a bore I shall explain it, its relevance will become clear later.

The drugs act on the electrical circuitry of the brain and on the soft penumbra of the brain cells. They do not effect the errant mind as such, a mind is not physical and cannot be affected by drugs. However they increase, for a time, the lines of communication between the other minds, thereby suppressing the influence of the errant mind. But the effect is temporary.

In the end all the drugs have done is cause permanent damage to the communicators and cells within the brain, and the patient is left less able to cope effectively than before—the longer the drug therapy the worse the damage. The short period of clarity is dearly bought.

Now that I have gotten that off my nonexistent chest, I can go on.

When a human's disharmony is caused by an errant mind there is only one effective therapy—love. The mind must be persuaded that living is not a disaster. No amount of rationalizing will help. It does not help a three-year-old in a tantrum to rationalize, his or her minds are not yet ready to understand rationalizations. Nor is a mind alone able to rationalize.

Your dog, Spot, responds best to love, it is something that his one mind can take in and understand. In a suicidedly depressed human we are dealing with one, or more, individual minds that are determined to make their exit from life. Remember that they are single minds! They are acting singly. They cannot think as a normal consciousness, only react.

As errant minds they are reacting to traumas of the past—either in this life or in a previous one. But however they react, the cure is the same. Love the minds.

How do you love an errant mind? How do you love your dog, or your cat? You hold it, you talk to it calmly, you stroke it. You demonstrate your love. You do the same with a baby.

It is not easy. You are doing the work of All There Is and it is not easy! It is by no means easy to love something that would destroy you! Turn it over to your persona. Turn it over to me.

Give me your depression as a gift. Think of wrapping it as a present, tying it with a bow and giving it to me. At first you may laugh at the suggestion! Why would I want your depression? What foolishness, you say!

But your depression comes from you whom I love.

How can I not welcome it? Do you reject the finger painting of a young child because it is not beautiful to an adult? Of course not! You take it and you love it because it is part of the child you love.

You are the child of All There Is and I am here to take your present on behalf of All There Is and to give you love in return. And to give your errant mind love. And I will do this over and over. I will accept the tantrums and I will accept the despair.

FIFTEEN — INTERNAL DISHARMONY

The nuclear family is, by its very nature, dysfunctional. Even in the happiest families there can be tension, depression and addiction. This has to be realized if you are to rid yourself of guilt. You cannot *make* a family happy.

How often have you heard the absurd phrase 'working on a marriage?' How many couples have you known go into therapy to try to 'make their marriage work?' The underlying assumption behind all this nonsense is that a nuclear family can work if only.......! (Fill in the space yourself, it matters not.)

Coming from this is the notion of failure—somebody within the family has failed. The most tragic result of this is when the children of the marriage believe that it is they who have failed. The guilt arising from this will last throughout their lives.

Psychologists have made a living out of this guilt from the time of Freud on and some, the more understanding ones, do some good in dealing with the frightened child within the adult. The rest merely go over old ground ad nauseam to no avail because they do not realize what the real problem is.

The basic problem is not the people in the family but the institution itself! One man working alone cannot bear the responsibility for the family's welfare. One woman cannot be expected to bear the entire brunt of child raising. Two working parents deprive the children of family itself.

Your economic and religious systems made the nuclear family, your society has crushed its members! Even the case of a man raping his four-year-old daughter has its roots in that man's inability to find self-esteem and control within the system your kind has created.

So let us hear no more about failure within the family. It will take time to overcome this notion. You have societal prejudices to overcome, religion, the state, the financial system—all the organs of repression have a stake in your feelings of guilt. But you will give it to me, and I will relieve you of it.

That you live in a competitive society instead of a cooperative tribe is not your fault—really! Your disharmony springs from the impossibility of the situation and your attempts to cope with it.

Addiction (of which I will talk later) springs largely from an inability to take the responsibility that the nuclear family imposes.

Addiction leads to guilt as the children of the addict try to rescue their addicted parent and of course 'fail.' They try to hide that addiction from the outside world and grow up feeling unable to make friends because of the fear that some unnamed 'something' will come out and ruin the friendship.

That the financial failure of the parents should bring harm on the children merely shows how dysfunctional your whole society has become. Listen to me, please, the harmony of your very soul depends on your understanding what I am saying.

YOU ARE INNOCENT! YOU ARE INNOCENT! YOU ARE INNOCENT!

SIXTEEN — INTERNAL DISHARMONY TWO

It is better if you carry out this part of the second step in the company of others; you may want their comfort as well as mine.

This may not be an easy journey.

I know that you have suffered. Give that suffering to me. Think of the times in early childhood that there were problems in your family. See yourself torn between your parents, or your siblings, as you competed for favor.

Realize that I am in your mind and I see the memories as they arise. Lie there and relax, don't hold your consciousness back. Feel yourself to be safe and in my embrace. It is important that you feel this safety and comfort because otherwise the memories can hurt you.

Give me your earliest memory. Your very first. Now give me the first image you have of your mother and your father. Are they smiling? Can you feel their love? You may not, you may feel instead their disharmony. Give that to me.

Close your eyes for a moment and let the memories flow. You are safe. Let your memories stay in your early years. Let them come, good or bad. Take your time, I am here for you however long it takes.

Think of the things that you possessed in those early years. Remember your relationship to those things—the toys, the house, the clothes. Feel again the importance that you felt those things had for you.

Focus in on one possession that you loved. See it in your consciousness. Give it again the love you had. Imagine now its love for you. Let yourself! Then you were confident of its love, you clung to it for comfort. Now realize that that was the love of All There Is being given to you through that possession.

Hold that image in your consciousness. Make friends with it. Talk to it if you wish. That will be a safe haven as we go on. Remember that that object loved you on behalf of All There Is.

Give me your first embarrassment. It is perhaps painful. Whatever it is give it to me. What was the role of your parents in that episode? Do not block anything. Remember I am ascribing no guilt to your parents. They too are innocent. Give it to me.

If pain comes, go back to the possession you loved. Remember you are safe in the space I have created for you. You are loved.

Just let memories flow and come in that dark, safe, loving space which is me. Rest and relax until it is time to go on. You will go down this path many times before you are ready to continue.

SEVENTEEN — BEING ALONE

There are many words which your kind uses—loneliness, being alone and so forth—words that express your feeling at being cut off from the closeness of other humans. You have created a society that praises the ability to be alone, a society that is increasingly structuring itself so that literally antisocial behavior—working from home, home shopping, home banking, drive-through restaurants etc. etc.—is the norm.

Let me say at once that there is something wrong with the individual—be it human or other—who does not savor the company of others. If the society or the family creates people who live alone, then there is something wrong with the family or the society.

A person cannot develop alone. A child cannot grow up alone. Sanity and harmony lie in group effort, group endeavor. That is true no matter what the circumstances.

Loneliness—being alone—leads to disharmony. Society must be structured in such a way that no member of it can be an outcast. But what you have now is a society of outcasts! Walk any of your streets and see! Drive down roads lined with walled estates, how absurd!

On starting life a baby should see many welcoming faces greeting its birth—not just its parents! Birth should be a family or tribal affair, and remember what I have said about the family.

The ending of life should also be a community event. No soul should have to leave this life alone! But so it is with all phases of life. Of course an individual must have his or her privacy. Naturally. Privacy is also necessary for harmony. But privacy should be voluntary.

I want to stress, while we are doing this second step, that you cannot achieve harmony if you are lonely. All of my cocooning will be of no avail if there are no others around you to share your experiences with.

Of course in one very important sense you are never alone. You are a part of All There Is and you cannot ever be completely alone. You also have your own persona who is with you all the time, and you will make contact with that entity.

I realize that, in the long term, your kind must abolish the nuclear family and restructure your society to mirror the new (though actually very old) concept of the family, or tribe. Later I am going to tell you how this can be achieved. But for now seek out others to accompany you on this journey to harmony. They will become your tribe, they will become whole.

EIGHTEEN — THE MANTRA

I give my life to All There Is.
I give my will, which is free, to All There Is.
I will be one with All There Is.

You are now ready, with your companions, to understand this mantra which I give you.

Before now you would have thought it a prayer, which it is not; or an invocation, which it is not; or a demand from the Universal Consciousness, which it is not.

The key to understanding these lines lies in the second—the words 'which is free.' All There Is requires nothing of you except the opportunity to bring harmony into its own consciousness, of which you are an integral part.

Your free will is essential to the working of your universe. To give it to All There Is is a way of saying that you wish to join in the harmony that is being created by bringing harmony to yourself.

You give your life to this process. You do not have to do anything, it is rather what you will become. You allow

All There Is, through your persona, or myself, to lead you to this harmony. To be one with All There Is is to enter into the harmony which is being created.

You must remember that you are not talking of, or to, a being outside of yourself. The paradox is that you are a part of All There Is and the harmony you seek already exists within you.

In a sense, when you speak the words of the mantra you are talking to yourself. I realize that this sounds odd to those who have had a religious upbringing. You see God as a controlling entity in the sky. Let me say that All There Is controls nothing, any more than you control your dreams. All There Is is only love unfolding and ridding itself of imperfections.

To say the mantra is to enter into love, to fall in love with existence, to wish to be one with that feeling, to wish never to be alone, to dissolve into the consciousness of All There Is.

Whenever you say the words you bring yourself closer to All There Is, and to your persona, or me. It is as if you reach out your hand when your own consciousness is frightened, alone, disharmonious, and it is taken.

In the depths of your despair the words will come and lull you into my cocoon. I wish nothing more for you at this stage of our journey than your ability to make that first gesture—the words, the hand.

NINETEEN — THE FAMILY AND SOCIETY

I am going to digress here. It is the prerogative of a persona to digress and you will not be able to understand what I have to say later if you have not read this.

I have already said something about the desirable family, or tribe. I want to now, briefly, say something about its relationship to society as a whole. Remember that a tribe is a unit that shares several basic characteristics:

First, it is cooperative and not competitive.

Second, it consists of a number of adults and children, not just one couple and their dependents.

There is nothing in this to say that it is territory-based, although all members should live in the same district.

If this, then, is the family, or tribe, how should a society be structured? Simple: just like that. Each family must be a society. For harmony to exist there must be no larger social units.

Immediately I see you raise objections—how could there be mass transportation? science? trade? without the larger units to regulate and organize these things. Again the answer is simple: by cooperation between families. Anything that cannot be done through this cooperation is disharmonious.

If you cannot build a road from coast to coast without a nation state to build it, then do not build it. If you cannot travel from continent to continent without some impersonal corporation to provide the transport, then do not travel. If you cannot finance development projects without the aid of non-family based institutions, do not develop.

In fact you will find that you will not lose many of the benefits of your civilization by structuring your society on the basis of a series of cooperating tribes. What you will lose is the need for control.

That is most important. Much of your disharmony comes from the need of others to control your lives. The larger a society gets the more the need for control becomes evident and the less the citizens of that society feel that they have the ability to organize their own destinies.

Naturally, the question arises as to how the system would work—when I explain this in detail you will be surprised how simple it all is. But for now, know that you do not live either in a harmonious society or within harmonious families.

TWENTY — CREATING A FAMILY

I said earlier that it is very difficult to successfully complete this journey to harmony alone, that you cannot bring up children as they should be brought up alone, that you need the support of others of your kind at every stage of your life.

Of course the ideal is to have a loving and harmonious tribe around you. But these families have ceased to exist. The nuclear family is very much part of the problem, and other extended families are ground down by the prevailing social structures to such an extent that they are, usually, just as useless.

So, what is to be done?

First, let me ask: What is a family?

The answer usually entails blood kinship. I reply that this is not necessarily so. Let me say, immediately, that I am not advocating a commune or an ashram. I am attempting to create families, or tribes, from scratch.

Let me then define this start-up tribe: It is a group of people who wish to cooperate together, who live in the same locality and who believe that the highest good is their own harmony. Nothing else matters. Look for no further commonalities.

Do not seek to define permanent roles within this family that you are creating. Certainly there should be no head of the tribe. If you create such a position you are merely aping the society you are seeking to replace.

How, then, are decisions to be made within the group?

By consensus. Nothing more. No votes, no dicta, no tyranny by the majority against the minority or vice versa.

Oh, it is not easy at first. You still have the disharmony of your upbringing to contend with and most of you are still working within the old social structures in order to bring in money. Some will drop out. Love them and let them go.

Gradually more families will arise and, in the second generation, become more established. Links will be formed between the tribes and the existing state will be bypassed, become irrelevant.

Of course it will take time, but that is not important. What is important for you now is that you will have created a family within which you can achieve harmony within yourself and with All There Is. You will have people around you to love and to be loved by. I will be with you.

TWENTY-ONE — TRUST

You who are disharmonious within yourselves find it hard to trust. It is hard for you to trust principally because your society is built on lies—lies proclaimed by the state, by your religions, by your parents, by your lovers and by yourselves.

The third step toward harmony is to learn to trust yourself and your persona.

In doing so you will be able to sort through the various levels of truth and realize that it is possible to accept some falsities as necessary to survive in a society such as yours. You will then be able to trust those who are seeking harmony but who, at the same time, attempt to protect themselves and those around them by some dissembling.

The biggest lie, after all, is the one you tell yourself —that you are not innocent and that you cannot be worthy of the love of All There Is. I tell you that that is a lie!

Trust brings harmony and distrust brings disharmony. For a disharmonious society to survive it must encourage distrust, and so it does. Distrust is part of the power of the state and all the other organs of control. You can overcome that distrust by learning to see through it.

First, assume that every person or organization that wishes to influence your actions is lying to you. Accept only the words of those who do not want or need control. Even if they are false, they cannot harm you.

This is difficult to accept, I know. If you are disharmonious you want a solid rock to stand upon, not the shifting sands of prevarication.

I am not advocating falsehood! Rather I am asking you to look for harmony. No person in your society—none!—can be totally honest. It is simply not possible. Your conventions, laws, regulations, philosophies and religions require lying!

To lie in order to do harm is wrong absolutely because it breeds disharmony both in the liar and in his or her victim. To lie to exert control is wrong absolutely for the same reason. Everything else is a variable and depends on the disharmony created by the falsehood.

Until you throw off this society you have created to imprison yourself in you will not have truth. But you can have trust.

First, trust yourself. As you can truly love no other until you love yourself, so you can trust no other until you trust yourself. I trust you. Those who know me I trust. I will lead you to trust in others.

TWENTY-TWO — TRUST AND LOVE

Let me say at once that you cannot have love without trust.

Some of you will immediately conjure up instances in which you have loved unwisely or in which you have loved in spite of a lack of trust.

In the first case let me say that when you love—anything or anybody—you create harmony, both internal and external. That harmony never dies, nor does the love. Once you have loved a person, for example, you never stop loving them. Never. You love all your past loves now, even when you imagine that you hate them. Hate is only a perversion of love, a crying out for the real thing.

But when you loved, first you trusted. Not in every way, perhaps, since your society does not allow for complete honesty, but in a way acceptable to you.

Love and trust always go together. To love yourself you must trust yourself.

But there are degrees of trust and there is only love. There are some of your kind who are, on the face of it, wholly untrustworthy—most of your politicians, for example, and all of your religious leaders. But All There Is loves even them. How is that? The simple answer is that All There Is is capable of no other emotion, but simply is love. Humans are different and must trust to love.

Look at the three meanings you give the word trust: First, you say you trust someone, meaning that they will do you no intentional harm and will take care not to harm you unintentionally.

Then you say you trust somebody meaning that you believe what they say (bearing in mind that every one of your kind is a liar at some time).

Finally you say you trust someone to.......... In other words you believe that they will follow a certain predictable course of action. This last has nothing to do with love.

It is only the first definition that has any validity as far as human love is concerned. That kind of trust brings harmony. By acknowledging that somebody is trustworthy in that sense you are also acknowledging that they are worthy of love.

By being open to that kind of trusting you will also increase the number of those you love, and who love you in return. You will be increasing harmony for yourself and others.

TWENTY-THREE — TRUST AND THE FAMILY

ince you will be building families from scratch at first, you are now in a position to look a bit more closely at those with whom you wish to travel to harmony.

I have said that trust is the belief that a person will do you no intentional harm and at the same time take care not to harm you unintentionally. To only those people can you give your love. You must attract those sort of people to you by being open to receive their trust and their love.

A man or woman's highest good is his or her own harmony, but in order to achieve that he or she needs the love of others. To secure that love, he or she must trust in others.

A family built in this way is built on trust and on love and, inevitably, will be built on harmony. Trusting individuals cannot help but cooperate with each other, cannot but love each other, cannot but create harmony.

Contrast this to the present family system in which disharmony is created. There is love, often, yes. But that love is the love that was there, naturally, at the start of life because at birth there is trust. The new parents trust the infant, which is incapable of harming them and is therefore a fitting object of trust. The baby has no option but to trust the parents it has chosen.

The new families will be built on trust.

Not everyone you love and trust will become part of your family—by no means! It will take considerable time to build the group of like souls.

I use that word in its literal sense. You are joining souls. These souls will travel forward together to seek harmony in the next life and the ones after. I do not mean that they will always be humans belonging to the same family. That would be absurd because it would destroy the free will of the soul to become what it wishes to become. But the souls of the family will continue to be associated with each other—perhaps as master and pet for example—and share in each other's increasing oneness with All There Is.

For in essence that is what it is all about—being one with All There Is, seeking unity with the Universal Consciousness. That is the reason for love, for trust, for harmony, for families, for lovers, for pets, for a garden.

And for a persona.

TWENTY-FOUR — TRUST IN YOURSELF

 have said earlier that to love yourself you must trust yourself and in order to achieve harmony both within yourself and with All There Is, you must love yourself.

Trust yourself? It seems so easy! At first this request may seem trite and I ask forgiveness if that is the case. Most of you will immediately say that of course you trust yourselves. I can hear the chorus of 'The only person I trust is myself!'

I say that the mere use of that phrase proves conclusively that those in the chorus do not trust themselves. If you trusted yourself you would have the capacity to trust others. It is your own lack of self-trust that prohibits your opening up to others of your kind.

Let me put it this way: Remember, trust is a prerequisite for love. You must believe that premise. If you do not, let me ask you a question: Can you truly love someone you believe will do you ill? If you answer yes, then one or more of your minds is deceiving you and what you would feel is not love but self-hate—the desire to hurt yourself.

Assuming the answer is no, then you and I are one so far. Now, if trust is necessary for love the next question is: What else is necessary? I answer, nothing!

Of course you can trust another of your kind without loving them. But you cannot trust another of your kind without having the capacity to love them. The same is true of yourself.

That is the starting point. Admit, those who profess no self-love, that you do not trust yourselves either. You are utterly alone! You have no capacity to either love or trust another human being, especially yourself.

If you do not trust yourself, you cannot trust others.

If you do not love yourself, you cannot love others.

The clue to your (if you will pardon the phrase) salvation is this: You are loved by All There Is. Yes! Yes! Yes! The Universal Consciousness envelopes you and loves you.

Do not confuse this All There Is with Nature, which is not a being at all and which, at times, can be anything but benign. All There Is is the sum total of all the consciousness of all living things in your universe and in all others. And this consciousness loves you! There is love for you in every blade of grass, in every ant, in every elephant, in every bat, in every microbe and in every human. And in yourself!

TWENTY-FIVE — TRUST IN ALL THERE IS

Because All There Is is universal it is not logically possible to suppose that it means you harm individually. Even the most elaborate conspiracy theories could not go that far! And since the Universal Consciousness holds your existence in its mind, so to speak, you cannot imagine that it would cause you harm by neglect. Therefore you must trust it!

Wait! I hear the chorus again. The floods in Bangladesh! AIDS! Cancer! War! Oh dear!

Let us take those castastrophies:

The floods (or similar). Floods, earthquakes and other 'acts of God' are part of the way your planet regulates itself. All There Is cannot prevent them without destroying the very conditions that gave you the life you have. By choosing life, your soul was aware of the risks inherent in existence on this earth. It would not be sensible for you to distrust All There Is on the basis of natural disasters that are necessary for your kind to live!

AIDS. The AIDS virus is a living thing. In the eyes of All There Is its soul is as important as yours. It is mindless as an individual virus, though it takes on the semblance of a mind in the billions of the virus that infect your body or the untold trillions of them that exist in the world. Your kind, once in harmony, will be able to communicate directly with the viruses and work out a modus vivendi—a way of living together without mutual destruction. Look, your death is a disaster to any virus that inhabits your body. All There Is offers you a way of obtaining harmony and the eventual freedom from disease.

War. War, murder and so forth are acts of free will, the free will of every participant. In a state of harmony there can be no war. All There Is offers you freedom from these self-inflicted human ills.

Now you can see that these things are not causes to distrust All There Is. If you can trust All There Is, you can return the love of All There Is. But since you are part of All There Is, you are, in effect, trusting and loving yourself!

Oh, I hear another chorus! Yes, you say, I can love All There Is but I still cannot love myself. What you say is a trick!

I tell you that if you can admit to the love of All There Is you are well on the way to self love. If you can trust in All There Is—even in the most neutral way—then you can trust yourself.

Now! Take the first step. Say 'I am willing to trust All There Is.' Again! 'I am willing to trust All There Is.' Again! 'I am willing to trust All There Is.' Good. Now I need not tell you what the next phrase to say is. Say it! Good. We go on together.

TWENTY-SIX — INTERMISSION

I am going to have a station break. During this break I get to talk about something other than harmony, All There Is and all that.

I want to talk about grass and a blue sky and the shimmer of bare branches in a winter wind and the unimaginable colors of a coral reef. I want to talk about the things I like to think about. Even a persona can have preferences.

I am sometimes asked what I am thinking about and I answer 'Everything,' and that is true. Everything encompasses the past and the future and the present and everything that exists, existed or has the potential to exist.

But I do not think about all things equally. Your kind think of seven things at once with your seven minds, but only onc or two rise to the level of consciousness. So it is with me. I like to watch the development of a blade of grass and marvel at the beauty of its whole being. Yes, even I can marvel. I wonder do you know how many colors there are in a reef?

Oh, I know that the divers amongst you will tot off reds and blues and greens and grays on the fingers of your hands and the toes of your feet. But that is only because you are looking through your eyes.

Add to this the colors that a shark sees, and a moray eel, and a sea anemone and the totally different range of hues seen by those creatures your scientists proclaim to be color-blind. There are a billion and more shades of blue alone seen by the creatures I have mentioned. Is it any wonder that I, who see them all, have preferences in my thoughts?

The stark branches of a winter tree rattling in a stiff breeze stand out in my thoughts. The blue of the sky behind them is so pale compared with the rich blue of summer — even to your sight. So many of your kind do not look up to see.

I am enjoying this intermission.

Look at a virus. The complexity of this small universe is worth thinking about. You can hold a trillion of them in a glass of water yet each has a soul like yours. And each soul has beauty and has chosen this form of life and each is worthy of thought.

And then there is you. You who are beautiful and complex beyond your own belief, you whom I have chosen to guide. You are uppermost in my thoughts, even when I think of everything. Even when I think of the colors of the reef, or the tree in winter, or the wonder of the soul of the virus. You hold within you the potentiality for the harmony of a universe. Are you not amazing? Thank you for the station break.

TWENTY-SEVEN — TRUST AND YOUR PERSONA

Strange as it may seem it is easier to trust your persona than it is to trust yourself.

It is easier to sink into me, to let yourself go utterly, than it is to face the fact that you are worthy of your own trust. Very well, then, sink into me. Let me hold your minds and your soul as gently as I would a feather as it drifts slowly through infinity.

Let me enfold your whole being as if I were a loving parent. Feel arms around you, caressing you, caring for you. Release yourself to me.

Let go of your fears, they are empty shells from your past. Let go of your present worries, they are nothing and will pass. Let go of your body for I am holding it. Finally let go of your soul.

Let me hold and cherish you entirely. I am a link between you and love, the love of All There Is. I will not leave you or desert you. I cannot let you down because all I have to give is love. I love you because I will and not because I must.

Now sink deeper into me. Here your eyes see nothing but infinity, a void of nothing except the one unfolding emotion that drives this and every universe. Feel me stroke you. Yes, you can feel the physical sensation even though I have no physical presence.

I say I love you. Lean on the words and cling to them. Search the meaning. Linger over the phrase. Taste it like the specialty served up by a master chef, All There Is is a master chef and love is his speciality.

It is this love that you crave, undemanding, unending, unconditional. And you have it, now, while you rest within my being and allow me to hold you.

I see a small panic in your minds—what happens when I am not holding you? Rest easy, that love will be with you always. It will be there for you to rely on, to fall back on, to trust.

And I trust you. Accept that whilst you are safe within my caress. I trust you. I trust you. Let those words sink into your consciousness, gently. As you are surrounded by love you are also surrounded by trust.

Now let some of that trust come through along with the love. It is all I ask. Take it for your own and let me share it with you. As you trust me to be there and love you, accept a little of my trust of you to be there and love me.

Now when you face your days and nights you will never be alone. I trust you to trust yourself. I trust you to love me. I trust you to love yourself. As you trust me you will learn to trust your own persona for we are the same. Never forget that you have a being such as I to guide you and to love you and to care for you, if you will allow it. Trust me, you will.

TWENTY-EIGHT — YOUR PAST

The reason for your disharmony lies, in good measure, in your past. The next step toward harmony is to deal with your past, to face it, to analyze it and to see how it has affected you. This past is composed of a number of elements:

Your family history.
Your social position.
Your educational background.
Your spiritual life.
Your web of relationships.
Your past lives (if any).

Each of these will have contributed, in some measure, to the disharmony that you now experience. Remember, however, before we go on further, that you live in a highly disharmonious society and that this overall social malaise has affected you, perhaps, more than anything in your past.

Contrary to what some therapists and psychoanalysts say, not everybody is poisoned by their parents, no matter how disharmonious the relationship between them was. It is perfectly possible to be internally in harmony and yet come from addictive, abusive or unloving parents. It is wrong to blame everything on your parentage.

However it is very difficult to find your way to internal harmony if you have come from a disharmonious family. That is abundantly evident.

The same is true of your social position. It is hard to find peace within yourself if you were hungry, if every day was a struggle to survive, if you were not adequately nourished. But it is not only the poor who are disharmonious!

How difficult it is for anyone to live in harmony when there is suffering around them. Your society eats into the rich as well as the poor.

Then there is your educational background, your schooling. I have said before that your schools are merely prisons for your young. I do not believe that any one of your kind was helped along the road to harmony through imprisonment!

The religious teaching that you received will also have added to your disharmony. Falsehoods never brought harmony.

Your past relationships with other disharmonious people will have affected you greatly. And so will your past lives. I will deal with each of these over the next few pages. Bear with me, we are making progress.

TWENTY-NINE — YOUR PARENTS

Let me repeat something I have said before: A family consisting of only two adults is absurd! I have mentioned some of the idiocies that the concept of the nuclear family has led to. I want now to move a bit deeper.

Do not blame your parents for your disharmony, the fact that your family was dysfunctional was not their fault! You cannot come into harmony by carrying the burden of blaming those who brought you up.

Of course it is important to realize that the cause of your disharmony lies, to a large part, in them. It is important because you must rid yourself of the guilt that you feel. A child of a dysfunctional family will try to 'save' the family, feel it has a responsibility to hold it together—to prevent the divorce, to cure the addiction, to absorb the abuse.

You must realize that you are innocent. Totally. Absolutely.

But you must also realize that your parents are also innocent. There is no buck that stops! You can trace the dysfunctionality back through a million of your years. And at each stage there is confusion and innocence.

It will not help you to look for guilt, it is a futile and meaningless occupation and I absolve you of it.

Remember also that if you start a nuclear family, that, too, will be dysfunctional no matter how hard you try to make it otherwise. It, too, will add to the disharmony of your offspring no matter how kind, gentle and loving you are.

But you will be innocent of that disharmony! Totally. Absolutely.

You must grasp this because it is fundamental to everything that I have to say regarding harmony: Harmony will not come to your society as long as it is organized as it is with nuclear families as its base.

You must search your memory for all that happened in your childhood, the good and the bad. Relish the good. Give it to me, now. Those times are your gems. Like the plaything that you loved and which I spoke of before.

Now the bad. See how in the worst times your parents were torn by the position that they had been placed in. How they took their frustrations out on you. Of course they were wrong to do so, that is obvious, and you suffered. But look to the causes. Look to the causes.

Now, child, rest, and take my love, for the journey is difficult.

THIRTY — YOUR PARENTS TWO

When a child is born, he or she comes to parents that he or she has chosen. Never forget that this birth is an act of choice — not always on the part of the parents, but certainly on the part of the child's soul.

Yet the baby is invariably born into a stressful family situation. Even in the most harmonious of nuclear families, the arrival of a child is a very stressful event. Sometimes the problem is an extra mouth to feed in hard times, or the new arrival may symbolize, for one or both parents, the end of freedom and the dawning of an awesome responsibility.

And the responsibility is awesome.

Some parents are forced to deny this feeling, they believe that it is wrong to feel burdened. Your society simultaneously worships parenthood and makes it as difficult as possible.

This denial of the unwanted responsibility passes to the child who then feels guilt at being the cause of this problem. Do not believe that children cannot sense that they are a burden. This denial of the fear of responsibility is the first big lie that the infant will face. He or she will sense it from the crib.

As a parent you cannot avoid the sense of unwanted responsibility, no matter how much you love your child.

The feeling is smothered in phrases such as:'It is difficult to bring a child into this uncertain world.'

This is code for 'help!'

But there is no help available. There is a lot of pious and unwanted advice and a bureaucracy more intent on its own self-interest. But no help. The structure of society is such as to prevent help.

For the wage-earner (or earners) the new arrival means new sacrifices and harder work. For the mother, the choice between confinement and guilt.

And so it goes on throughout the period of childhood. Each new problem adds new weight to the burden of responsibility and guilt.

But, you say, don't some parents get great pleasure from their children?

Of course. Of course. But the deep reality is that few are able to escape the almost inevitable combination of responsibility and guilt. Only the creation of tribal families such as I have outlined earlier can save your kind.

THIRTY-ONE — SOCIAL POSITION

Inequalities in wealth are disharmonious! They are absurd!

I tell you that to have more or fewer possessions than another of your kind is like acid that eats at the fabric of your soul! You cannot be harmonious being either poor or rich.

While there is one hungry human on your planet your kind is condemned to disharmony and eventual, and premature, extinction.

Look, it is fine for you to drive an automobile, live in a decent house, talk on a telephone, use a computer, play with a toy. I would not stop you, these things bring pleasure. But what is the value in possessing them?

Does it really give you pleasure to drive a splendid car if another human being is denied any form of transport? If it does, then that only shows how deep disharmony goes.

I am not saying that every one of your kind <u>must</u> have an automobile. That would be absurd. But there must be choice. Cars must be available if they are needed.

Oh I know you are thinking that this is socialist nonsense. ATI has finally broken down. Poor old fellow. Pity.

But I am not a socialist. I do not want the state to have anything, much less everything. I do not want states at all. I want families who share what they have—the rewards and the burdens.

Every existing society has a class structure. A class structure denies the full humanity of each of the classes. Every existing society has leaders and a bureaucracy—yes, even African bushmen have a tribal bureaucracy—and those led in your societies are treated no better than household pets, at best. For harmony to come this absurdity must be swept away and buried.

Whatever your social position it has contributed to your internal disharmony and your inability to be at one with All There Is. You are denied the love that is your due.

The desire for possessions is natural in your society. Do not feel guilty because you feel it. I do not want your impoverishment and harmony is not helped by that. I want you to see not your own failings, but the absurdity of the society in which you live. I do not advocate that you give away what you have, but rather that you strive to create the family structure that will take over from the nation state.

THIRTY-TWO — SOCIAL POSITION TWO

hat is a society for? I tell you that there are four reasons for your living in concert with others of your kind:

Child rearing.

Cooperation for food and shelter.

Companionship.

Harmony.

In reality they are not separate, and were never meant to be. They are all aspects of cooperation. It does your planet no good to have competition between members of your species. Competition leads to disharmony.

Ideally you should be part of a small cooperative unit which has mutually cooperative relations with other units. The units, which I refer to as families or tribes, would not be exclusive and inward-looking for this would soon lead to rivalry between families and they would become just like so many warring clans.

Rather, social and commercial interaction between them would be the norm. Because neither would have territory there would be nothing to defend or to conquer. Rather than a dispute over water rights, for example, the first question should be: 'How can we organize our families so that the water is shared?'

This may seem so obvious as to be trite. Perhaps. And of course there are strong objections to this simplistic notion. Good.

But what would happen if harmony were the norm and the objections were not raised? If indeed it was normal to be in harmony with other families and within your own family, then the objections to cooperation would be as absurd-sounding as the idea of cooperation is now simplistic-sounding.

Yes, yes. I know. You ask: 'What about now?' Now, when there is internal disharmony racing through your seven minds and the world you live in is very far from being a collaborative place?

That is just my point. Reach out. Form families. Try. Forget the flower-power and the drug-induced communes of the sixties. Forget the utopian, exclusive, communities of 19th century socialists.

Find those with whom you would like to travel to harmony. Those with whom you would like to unite to face the raging disharmony all around you. Find them and love them. Love them because they share your search. That is a start. That is a fine start.

THIRTY-THREE — SPIRITUAL LIFE

I can hear you saying it! Education is coming! Wait, children, wait. The problem of education is the most difficult of all to grasp and there are things I must impart first.

I want now to talk about how your kind's spiritual quest has led to disharmony.

Belief in a god outside of yourself was the original cause of disharmony in your species. Everything negative that you feel — the guilt, the separation, the loneliness, the inadequacy — stems from that.

First let me emphasize the following: There is no God that you can pray to. There is no God that will punish you. There is only All There Is, the Universal Consciousness, of which you are a part.

This is how it happened, this absurd notion of external gods. At first your kind assumed that they were part of everything and felt the connection with everything. Loneliness was unheard of, fear of death was unknown, rivalry was not even contemplated, life was long.

Then fire was invented. A useful invention and, like most inventions, harmless in itself. But those who were designated the keepers of fire began to enjoy the power that position gave them. To further bolster their position they invented a God of Fire whom they alone could propitiate.

As this God was external to your kind, the belief in it automatically meant that the believers felt cut off from All There Is.

Soon there were gods for everything—a ludicrous pantheon of water gods, tree gods, monkey gods, mountain gods, sea gods, thunder gods and so on and so on and so on.

The rites and rituals surrounding these deities became more elaborate as each god and his attendant priests competed for believers. Humankind was separated from part of themselves—the divine.

But harmony cannot survive in this isolated state. I swear to you that you cannot be in harmony if you see the divine as anything other than within you. Your consciousness is part of The Consciousness. You are part of All There Is.

How can you hate your fellows if you see that, in reality, you are the same? You are not your brother's keeper, you are your brother. The spoon you eat with and you are the same. The food is part of you before it even enters your mouth. The steer is part of you before you kill it, the rice before you pick it.

How absurd, then, to have these gods. Or even God singular in any external sense. When you become at one with All There Is you are, in a very real sense, becoming at one with yourself. Remember that.

THIRTY-FOUR — WAIT A MOMENT

Oh dear! ATI is about to go into another intermission, and so soon after the last! Not a bit of it.

I want to take a moment, as your persona or your persona's representative, while we are on the subject of spirituality, to clear up a few questions that might become concerns.

First: Are we starting a church or sect? And if so, won't that lead to the twin evils of belief and disharmony?

It would, if we were, but we aren't, so it won't.

You do not have to believe in your persona, it exists anyway. There are two meanings of the word belief, and perhaps I had better clarify what I mean by belief in this context.

If you say that you believe that one and one make two, you are making a true statement. The truth of the statement, and therefore the reason for the belief, lies in the definition that your kind has given to the word 'two.' It is inconceivable, given that definition, to imagine any universe in which the statement that one and one make two would be false.

But the statement: 'I believe in a persona,' is quite different. It is perfectly possible for you to imagine a living entity - yourself, for example, that does not have a persona. It is not inherent in the definition of the word 'persona' that it is a link of anything to anything.

And if the statement is not true in the same way as one and one making two is, you should doubt it.

Therefore we are not trying to make anyone believe in anything.

This leads to the second question: If you are not asking us to believe in you, how can you expect us to believe that you can help us?

In fact the very words of the question are its answer. If I tried to make you believe, I could never bring you the comfort you need. I do not expect you to believe in me or my help. I ask you to let go and receive it.

Well, if it's not a church or a sect, what is it? Ah! Yes! what indeed?

We are starting a family, a tribe. One such as your kind has not had for millions of years. It is the prototype of many that will bring your entire species back to harmony. Nothing more and nothing less. It is not a church for the worship of a god, it is not a sect with beliefs. It is a family brought together because its members wish to journey to harmony one with the other. With me.

THIRTY-FIVE — YOUR RELATIONSHIPS

Now that we have gotten the bit about belief out of the way for a moment, let me get back to your past.

Ever since you were born you have developed relationships with others of your kind. Some of these have been rewarding and others not. Some have increased the sum of your harmony and others not. Those that involved love, of any kind, increased your harmony.

As I have said before, you still love all those you ever loved.

However all those whom you have come in contact with have come from dysfunctional homes, a disharmonious society, or both. You have taken from each some of that disharmony. Even those you have loved.

The deeper the relationship between you and one in disharmony, the more disharmony you take on.

In your society there is no escape from this situation. You are part of your society, your society is disharmonious, therefore you have to make contact with disharmonious people. In doing so you become less harmonious.

Remember: He or she who functions best in your

society is the least harmonious of all! To the extent that you find it difficult to cope with those around you, there is hope for you. (I will deal with the problem of a human with a malfunctioning brain later, I have already touched upon it but there is much more to say. I am not now talking about such people.)

It is in this view of sanity that I and the therapists part company. I do not want you to be able to function better in the society as it is. That would be absurd. You do not say to the drowning man: I will help you drown!

Of course not. You say: Here is my hand, take it, there is solid ground.

Realize, then, that from now on you will look at each relationship and ask this question: Is this person more harmonious than I? If the answer is yes, then you ought to allow a relationship with that person. If the answer is no, do not.

This is important and extends even to your choice of check-out clerk in a supermarket. Every contact is a relationship. The disharmony you get from the wrong clerk is far worse than being overcharged, accept that! Now, go in peace, and be the one your kind chooses to form ties with.

THIRTY-SIX — RELATIONSHIPS TWO

Let us look a bit more deeply into relationships. Perhaps more deeply than your kind has so far looked.

Let me repeat that a meeting, no matter how fleeting, is a relationship and that the effects of it will remain with you throughout this life and, perhaps, through several lives.

What happens when you meet another being (for we are talking about any sentient creature, not just your own kind)? Several things occur on different levels.

First, your minds come into contact.

Second, there is an exchange of biological and genetic information.

Third, there is contact between souls.

Finally, there is conscious contact.

Each of these is complex and could take up an entire book, but I will spare you that. It is, however, worth delving a bit into each because if you are to choose harmonious relationships you ought to know what a relationship is.

What does it mean 'minds in contact?' I hear you now saying that ATI is going to list several meanings and confuse the issue. You will be relieved to know that I am only going to list two.

There is an electrical communication between the brains of the two meeting individuals that is sparked, if you like, by their minds (I have discussed this when talking earlier of illness).

And there is an analysis by the minds of the incoming electrical information.

Each mind gives its total life history to the other individual's minds. If the contact is between two humans, there is mind-reading by fourteen minds. Most of this information does not come to the surface of the consciousness except as a general 'first impression' of the other individual. Because this 'first impression' is based on the total information of the other individual's minds, it is usually the best guide to what the other person is really like.

You instinctively know if a dog is dangerous, if a cat is friendly, if a human is trustworthy. You know this because you do, in fact, 'know.' By learning to rely on this knowledge you can select to develop relationships with those people who are most harmonious.

You all have this skill, you are all mind readers!

THIRTY-SEVEN — RELATIONSHIPS THREE

ow we are going to be even more controversial. I have said that at each meeting there is an exchange of biological and genetic information. Let me explain.

At the start of each meeting there is usually some physical contact — a handshake, a kiss, an exchange of a physical object — this contact allows the two bodies, human or other, to exchange biological and genetic information.

For example, take a hand-shake.

The friction of the movement of skin-on-skin forces some molecules of the outer skin, which is continuously being shed in any case, to be left on the opposing hands. That skin is absorbed by the bodies of the hand-shakers along with their genetic code, some of the viruses they carry and so forth.

The same is true of the rub of a nose, the lick of a dog's tongue, or an accidental jostle.

Your minds immediately analyze this information and process it. For example when a man and woman meet and shake hands the information exchanged will tell their ages, their state of health, their propensity to sire or bear children, their racial background, their likely longevity. Everything needed, in fact, for biological mating.

Clever, isn't it?

Of course, you object, it is quite possible for a relationship to begin on a mental level alone without any physical contact—with a telephone conversation, for example. Surely in this case there is no such information exchange?

Granted, the level of information received is much less in this instance, but it is still there. Your voice carries a great deal of biological information within it. The timber of it tells your age, for example, the wavelength used carries your racial mixture, your height, weight and so forth.

Naturally, not all this information comes to the surface consciousness correctly. Your minds may misinterpret what they receive due to the information being filtered through your own concerns and dysfunctionality.

So what does this mean practically? It means, for example, that you should never agree to do anything with anyone you have not met personally. To find harmonious souls you must, without exposing yourself to the risk of disease or other dangers, make physical contact with each of the candidates. Shake hands with the person, pat the dog, stroke the cat. Each of these actions will bring you to a better understanding of the other being you are making contact with.

In some societies the initial contact, it may be argued, involves no physical connection at all. It may be that it is with a mutual bow rather than by a handshake. The result may not be as effective, but the principle is the same. The biological reason for this form of greeting (as opposed to any sociological reason) is that the bow brings the heads of the persons closer together and makes it easier for the minds, through the brains, to interrelate. In the same way, when subjects bow to their monarch they are in fact exposing their minds to the gaze of those of the monarch.

THIRTY-EIGHT — WHEN SOULS COLLIDE

Well, of course, they don't actually physically collide. Something without substance cannot collide with anything, least of all another something without substance. But in a certain sense they do.

When you meet another being—sentient or not—your soul and the soul of the other being do come into contact. This contact is very subtle, and I do not want to place too much emphasis on it.

I have said that, during life, a soul is somewhat inactive—life, for it, is a passive experience no matter what form of life it chooses. Nevertheless a soul will feel the effect of the first meeting and any developing relationship and, sometimes, will make direct contact with the other soul. This contact is difficult to explain in human terms because you demand precision and in this instance there is none. But I will try.

Remember that a soul, in life, uses the minds of the being it is giving life to (assuming that being has any) whereas in the other existence it uses the Universal Consciousness directly. When contact is first made the soul absorbs the information brought to it by the mind or minds through whatever senses are working (plants work differently, but that is beyond the scope of this book).

Occasionally a soul will want more information than this process is able to provide , or it may want to bypass the filters through which the information passes. Then it will try to make direct contact with the other soul.

This contact comes as an exchange of love—not sensual, not romantic, not intellectual. It asks a simple question: Can the disharmony in this being's soul harm the being I inhabit, or myself?

This is, obviously, a vital question. Unfortunately, unlike the minds, which react quickly to the meeting, the soul takes its time. Remember that a soul does not view time in the same way your consciousness does, so taking its time could be long or short in your terms. A soul, being eternal, is in no hurry and does not feel the constraint of time. The answer may come quickly or over a number of your years.

But, if the answer is that the other soul is harmonious, then a relationship can be forged which will last a lifetime and is indissoluble.

This, then, is the true 'compatibility' which you strive for. It is the union of two souls. It may happen once, twice, or never in your lifetimes, but I would wish it for you.

THIRTY-NINE — PAST LIVES

I am still not ready to deal with education, or to be more honest, you are not ready to deal with your educational background. We have a little way to go. For now I want to make it clear that the roots of your present disharmony do not lie, to any great extent, in your past lives. There are those who say that the function of the soul in being reborn is to expurgate itself of wrongs committed in past lives. This is nonsense!

This is not to say, however, that you do not carry with you some of the disharmony resulting from experiences of past existences.

How does something that happened to you in a past life affect the soul, since the soul has no memory? Ah! This is a difficult question and begs a further question—doesn't it always?—What is memory?

There are three kinds of memory:

Existential, that which is a result of the experiences of your minds (this we will go into in some detail later).

Genetic.

Nonexistential (that is of the soul).

Existential memories deal with the memories of your

minds from the time your soul joined your body <u>and</u> memories they carry, sub-consciously, from other existences. I do not want to place too much emphasis on this latter, suffice it to say that your minds can carry memories, deeply buried, from past lives (not necessarily yours). These past existence memories normally have little, if any, effect on your present life.

Nonexistential memories deal solely (excuse the pun) with harmony. A soul has no mechanism to remember particular events or lifetimes, but it can 'remember' (perhaps 'feel' is a better word, I do not know since we are dealing with things for which your kind has not invented words) the pain of disharmony which becomes an integral part of its being.

Look at it this way. If I write 'soul' on the page you recognize it immediately. It is a soul correctly spelled. Let us assume 'soul' is harmonious. Now if I write 'soull,' you will still recognize it. Again 'sgoull' is somewhat dyslexic, but still soul basically. We can get to '*shgoull@' and still, with a bit of detective work, figure out that 'soul' is what is meant.

Now assume, the l,g,h,@ and * were added as a result of disharmony in different lives. You see they fundamentally change the 'soul,' become an integral part of it, like blisters. This rather awkward analogy is the closest I can get to explaining the process whereby a soul takes on disharmony.

Of course, I know, I have not gone into any detail about genetic memory, but that is because it is not relevant to this particular discussion.

FORTY — BLISTERED SOULS

How do you know whether you have a blistered soul?

Almost certainly you have, unless you are a very young soul and have had no past lives at all. Since disharmony attaches itself to souls, and your kind has not yet developed a method of purging souls of disharmony, then it follows that you most likely have, to some degree, a disharmonious soul.

What does this mean in practice?

It means this: It will be almost impossible for you to lead a life free from internal disharmony. Quite apart from the ravages of your society and the legacy of your upbringing, you have this basic internal discord to deal with.

But why should a soul that has suffered through its experiences in life want to be born again?

This is the nub of it. A soul can only be stripped of its disharmony in life. As only life can create disharmony, so only life can recreate harmony. The soul will seek harmony through rebirth. But of course it must run the gauntlet, if it chooses a human life, of parents, society, schooling and so forth, all of which are potential creators of disharmony. If the life it chooses is non-human, then it is prey to disharmony inflicted upon it by humankind.

Harmony can only be achieved by a complete change in your society and a complete change within yourselves. In this I, or your own persona, can help by pointing you in the right direction. Once you have read and digested all that I have said you will be well on the way.

It works this way — first read and understand both the problem and the solution. Then take the first steps toward contacting your own persona. Start to follow the steps I am outlining to guide you toward internal harmony. At the same time gather around you the most harmonious people that you can to form a family. Next try to immerse yourself within that family as much as is practical; make it, in fact, your society. Encourage others to do likewise and interact with the families that they have formed. In other words, begin to by-pass the existing framework.

Your soul will become more harmonious through each step and your family will help to keep it so. In this way your soul will leave this life with fewer blisters than it began it with. Souls trying out this existence for the first time will not then become blistered with disharmony.

It is not easy, my children, but it is certain that this is the way your kind will go. Let me help you for the love I bear you, and for the love of All There Is.

FORTY-ONE — EXISTENTIAL MEMORY

I have already attempted to explain what a mind is, now I want to explain something about its capacity to store existential memories.

Mind and soul work this way: When a soul decides to become, say, a field mouse, it requires one mind for that mouse to become active. A mind is provided by the Universal Consciousness for that purpose. The soul and the mind become a sort of team and may well go on to become other creatures together. If the soul chooses to become a human then it will be accompanied by six other minds.

During life the minds collect, and store, experiences. Some of these are readily recalled—what you call the conscious memory. These memories relate only to this life. It is important to bear this in mind—the mind cannot bring to consciousness any memory of a past life at all. Those who claim to be able to summon up specific memories of past lives through hypnosis are fooling themselves and their unfortunate customers.

However the memories are there—buried and unobtainable. Their reflections create harmony or disharmony in the mind. But it is a pale reflection. If you are not in disharmony through other factors you will not be seriously harmed by these shadows.

Of all the causes of disharmony, vague memories of past lives are the least important; active and conscious memories of this existence are far more important.

There is, however, one caveat to this generalization. It occasionally happens that a mind has been so harmed by an event or events so terrible that it has become permanently damaged. That mind will never be brought into any sort of harmony and it will seek only the destruction of the being it is part of.

But even then your persona may be able to help. I will talk of that in greater depth at some other time. For now, peace.

FORTY-TWO — SUMMATION OF THIS PART

Now you have all the causes of your present disharmony except those that are genetic or result from a damaged brain. I have spoken of the disharmony created by your parentage, your society, your religious background, your education (very briefly, much more of this later) and so forth.

I want you to read this part of the book over and over again. I want it to sink in. I want you to recognize in each of the causes of disharmony those factors that apply to you. Spare nothing. Each day consider a new factor. Meditate upon it. Dredge your memory to see how you have been affected.

You cannot be harmonious until you recognize all the roots of your disharmony—otherwise they will stay there ready to sprout again. It will not be easy, this constant searching of the past for the wounds you carry.

Some of the causes of disharmony you can do very little about — for example your past lives. But the important thing is to recognize them and proclaim your own innocence and your own perfection.

After each contemplation say: I am innocent! I am

innocent! I am innocent! Then give yourself over to be loved by your persona and by All There Is. Realize that you are worthy of that love and that you have been grievously injured by forces outside your control. Gradually you will be cured of each of the inflictions I have spoken about.

Do not set yourself a timetable, because the mere setting of it dooms you to failure and to guilt. I, or your own persona, will be with you all the time as you go through this process. You will become more used to our presence and more used to the love we have for you.

PART THREE: FORMING THE FUTURE

ONE — FAMILIES

I have talked about the sort of families that I believe will come into being and the need for them. However I have not, so far, made a convincing case for them in terms that your kind can readily understand.

It is all very well for me to go on about the need for families in order to restore harmony, but that is not really convincing to one who is not convinced of the need for harmony in the first place. Let me tell you why the family system I have outlined is not only good but inevitable.

Your world is falling apart.

You have come to the place where the dominant ideology on your planet relegates your species to the role of mere consumers of goods and services. You feel that you are merely the sum total of what you possess. You have no idea of your role in the ecosystem. You tout the idea of freedom yet try to deny it to those who do not agree with you. You are at the mercy of mindless technology and fanatical beliefs. You can walk down one of your streets and pass by beggars, fearing to extend a hand to them lest they mug you in return. You cram your prisons full of unfortunates and wonder why the incidence of violent crime goes on rising. You are at the mercy of the state with its tentacles of bureaucracy controlling every aspect of your lives. You worship any god but yourselves. You demand more and more medicines yet sickness abounds. You praise the old but neglect them. You claim to love children but let them starve. You save waste and waste your lives.

Your planet can no longer support this sum of idiocies. Your states are irrelevant, your beliefs vacuous, your families disintegrating.

Does this tell you nothing? If I gave you a handful of dust and said: 'Go build a city!', the grains would slip through your fingers before you realized that the command was absurd. You wish to be led so much that you have lost the ability to use your own free will.

Truly you are innocents, children.

Listen, societies such as you have formed can no longer preserve your species. A world government, as proposed by some of your more simplistic thinkers, will only enmesh you in greater disharmony. If a small town cannot work under your present system, why should a world government? Men and women do not grow wiser with more authority!

So you need something else. What are the characteristics of the system you need? Thank you for posing the question in your minds, now we are getting somewhere! Come, let us move on together, you and I.

TWO — FAMILIES TWO

Included in the characteristics of a family such as will arise, besides those that I have mentioned earlier, are some that are necessary for your own preservation as a species. A family:

Must fit in with the ecosystem.

Must be internally harmonious.

Must be leaderless.

Must have no power structure.

Must have no force at its disposal.

Must be open, not closed.

Must be based on no rigid beliefs.

Must worship no external gods.

Must be cooperative internally and cooperate with other families.

Must respect individuality.

Must respect free will.

Must respect privacy.

These, then are the twelve ways by which you will know one of these families besides the fact that they are made up of people who choose to journey to harmony together and who are in the same general geographic locality.

O.K., so why are such families inevitable, if your kind wishes to prolong its existence? The answer lies in each of the characteristics. You can only live in harmony with your fragile ecosystem if you are internally harmonious. You cannot be internally harmonious if you feel that you are the object of coercion, if you cannot take charge of your life. Granted? Good! But you see each of the characteristics, then, is necessary because each takes away some present cause of disharmony in your present society.

I could demonstrate it with each one, but I feel that a little thought would do the job better.

But the question arises: These family-tribes may be all very well in theory, but won't humankind be the agent of its own destruction long before they come to pass? I will now answer that question.

THREE — FAMILIES THREE

You are with me, I am enjoying this!

Each species, including yours, will eventually seem to die out or evolve into something else, or both. The dinosaurs both died out in general and, at the same time, a small sub-species of them went on to become the birds that now populate your sky (when they are not sacrificed in the intakes of your jet engines). Since its inception humankind has been evolving, but the pace of biological evolution has not in any way kept pace with the rate of change in your societies.

No species dies out completely. (For the experts let me add this note: I know I seem to be misusing the term species. At times I am referring to genera as well as species. Bear with me, the distinctions are trivial in the scheme of things. Even given the distinction let me emphasize that no species has ever died out without first evolving its successor.)

The last major change in your species happened when Cro-Magnon man evolved, a mere 75,000 years ago. By the time of Neanderthal man, who arose about 400,000 years ago, your species had acquired both seven minds and the elements of disharmony through the worship of the god of fire. Cro-Magnons evolved separately from a common ancestor, and learned both the use of fire, and disharmony, from the Neanderthals. Both species were efficient hunter-gatherers and they are the fathers of all the races now on the earth. In some areas the Cro-Magnons wiped out the Neanderthals, in others the reverse happened. In some they fused.

So? You are still hunter-gatherers. So? So in order to survive you must have a society fit for hunter-gathers, yet not prone to the disharmonies that destroyed the earlier ones. The system of families is the only one possible. You cannot recreate the primitive (in the sense of early) Neanderthal or Cro-Magnon tribal lifestyle. There are too many of you and your technology is far too far advanced. And they were disharmonious!

You could destroy yourselves, but there is no possible future in which that will happen. However the ecosystem, the living planet, will not allow you to continue as you are going. You will soon come to the end of your ability to feed yourselves adequately. You cannot squeeze more from the planet indefinitely. You must change your ways. You must cooperate with the planet not rape it. But to cooperate with the earth you must cooperate with yourselves, internally and externally. You must, and will, develop a social system to do this. This system will be the new family structure.

FOUR — EDUCATION

I will return to families later—we have only just started to explore that subject. For now it is time I went on to that great cause of your own and your kind's internal disharmony, your educational system. At last! I hear you shout. I have left it until now because the future of your species demands a radical change in your educational methods.

Let me ask first (for here I am talking about schools for children, not other facets of learning): What is a school? Do not answer 'an educational institution,' for that is not an answer, only a misleading synonymous phrase. The elements in your system that define a school are:

A place where facts and information are imparted.

A place where the prevailing ideological and/or religious tenets of the society are proselytized and reenforced.

A place where children can interact with their peers.

A convenient place to deposit children while their parents work.

Educators will add to this list and attempt to take some of the items off the list. However a moment's passing thought will easily show that the above is the sum-total of a school's function (leave aside athletics and similar pastimes, for these could just as easily be followed outside of a school context).

I say that the only use of a school as it is presently set up lies in the last point—a prison for the children of working parents. It is a way in which your society increases its work force and thereby drives down the cost of labor so that useless things can be produced more cheaply!

I see you recoil in horror. ATI has finally gone mad! Very well, let us go deeper. Let me define a prison: A place where a person is incarcerated for a portion of his life against his will. Would you accept that? Good. That is what happens in school: We have established that a school is a prison. (I know it can be objected that many children actually like being at school. I would reply in two ways: First, they want to escape from disharmonious homes. Second, if they like school there is no need for compulsion.)

'Very well,' your educators retort, 'but it is necessary if the children are to learn.' It would be if it were, but it isn't, so it's not.

You have seven minds, use a few for a moment. The only thing that your minds do not know, at birth, is the future. That alone cannot be known. Everything else is memory. You do not have to teach a child biology—just allow him or her to follow the path of recollection. Under the right circumstances the interaction of your minds will bring forth any 'learning' that you need.

A great writer 'remembers' how to write, a mathematician 'remembers' his numbers, an inventor 'remembers' how to invent. But how? Now comes the interesting part!

FIVE — EDUCATION TWO

I do not expect that the majority of you will accept this theory of knowledge at once, but you will. Let me lead you, a bit, down paths that you will more readily accept.

A simple one-minded creature, such as a dog, comes into the world with a bundle of what you term 'instincts'—patterns of behavior that improve its survival and reproductive chances. These are often, but not always, reenforced by societal example. A snake, for example, knows how to stalk and kill its prey at birth. A turtle will return to the same beach to lay its eggs.

Now, I know that this latter can be argued to be a case of patterning—that the individual characteristics of the beach are programmed into the genetic fabric of the creature. Fine, I accept that. But that is simplistic. To say some behavioral characteristic is inherently genetic is to say no more than that it is stored, in some way, in the memory. However you define memory, you must accept that point—unless you arbitrarily exclude anything of your genetic inheritance from the definition.

So all minded creatures have a memory or (to be less

controversial, for you know how I eschew controversy) all creatures with a brain have memory. I can allow this point for I would say that a living creature that has a brain must also have one or more minds. So whether you use the term brain or mind in this context is irrelevant. O.K., so far?

Now, one step further and still no controversy. Any definition of knowledge must include that which is labelled 'instinctual.' A snake 'knows' how to kill, and what prey to kill; a shark 'knows' that it must move perpetually (not, of course all sharks—for the pedants); a bee 'knows' that it must combine with other bees to make a bee-city (the hive) and make honey (production); a humming bird 'knows' from which flowers it must get its nectar. Still with me? Good.

Each of these bits of knowledge aids in survival of course, and none of them are taught. Look at the complicated patterns of behavior that insects have—patterns that mirror, in almost every detail, your own.

The bee I spoke of has a language that consists, in its more overt expression, of the dance that tells other bees the exact location of sources of pollen, danger, and so forth. An ant lives in a society every bit as organized as your own. Most warm-blooded (and some cold-blooded) creatures have a family structure. And all without the benefit of schooling!

The next bit is going to be a mite more unacceptable to some; I caution educators with heart conditions to rest here.

SIX — EDUCATION THREE

One-minded (all right, small-brained, if you will!) creatures, then, can:

Function perfectly well in their environment.

Have a perfectly satisfactory family life.

Cooperate with others to build cities.

Engage in production.

Have a language.

And so on, and so on, and so on ad infinitum (literally). And they have all of this without jails and without disharmony! I might add that many of your own societies have managed to 'educate' their young without prisons.

'But,' the educators reply, 'the functions that the simple creatures are called upon to fulfill are much more rudimentary. Because we live in a more complicated world than they do, we need to draw on all the human experience of the past and to pass that on to our youngsters.' Rubbish!

Everything that a human child needs to survive, develop, and reproduce exists within his or her memory at birth. And if that is there then, why not more?

Why should the knowledge of city-creation be there

for an ant and not for a human? To say that the reason is because an ant needs the knowledge and a human does not is no answer. What about creative writing, then? Does not the art of writing need to be studied?

This latter raises a very important point. Of course, in your eyes, there are better and worse writers, better and worse painters, scientists, doctors etc. etc. Let me leave aside the definition of the word 'better' for now, since it is relative to the person who uses it. If you mean that the writer has a surer grasp of language, I would agree.

Still, however, the study that needs to be done is, essentially, one of memory. A child's interest in a particular field stimulates his or her minds to unlock more of the memory. Of course a child can be led to an interest by an enthusiastic adult (just as a sheep-dog can be led to be a 'better' herder). In most cases this willing and enthusiastic adult is a necessity.

Of course it will be argued against me that I am relying very heavily on this theory, as you would call it, of memory. What if I were wrong? What if knowledge were nurture rather than nature? Surely, the educationalists cry, it would be criminally foolish to throw out the entire educational system and rely on this far-out theory of memory?

I would agree. But I would contend that schools should be abolished whatever view you take about knowledge.

Where I differ from the run-of-the-mill educators is in the definition of what should be happening and where; for I fear that the more of your present education that you have, the more disharmonious your society becomes. I will explain.

SEVEN — EDUCATION FOUR

There are two strands in the development of children in your present society. First, there is the instillation of knowledge and second, there is the attempt to make the child accept the prevailing values of the society (I include within this second the values that enable the child to grow up and help contribute to its own and its immediate family's economic well-being).

The primary value that a school imparts is group loyalty. This may not be a conscious motivation of educators, but it is the natural result of the way the education system is structured. In this it is merely continuing trends that begin at the very earliest time of life.

A baby is an all-accepting thing (whereas an adult is, too frequently, an all-excepting thing!). In particular it accepts, uncritically, love from whomever is prepared to give it. In your present society, by the age of six months the child has begun to recognize those closest to it and to fear strangers.

Why? Fear of strangers is not instinctual in your kind. The reason for this early fear is simple—the baby is exposed to very few strangers! If you take the time to study the phenomenon of babyhood you will come to realize that the more loving people a child is exposed to at a very early stage in its life, the less it will grow to fear and hate strangers later on.

It is the beginning of the distinction between 'them' and 'us' in the child's mind.

The child moves on to school. There he or she finds a further limiting of the range of loving social interactions. The teachers are there to cram unwelcome facts down their captives' throats, the other pupils are ranged against the child in team sports, in class competitions, in examinations and so forth. Even so simple a thing as an inter-school baseball or football match reenforces 'them' and 'us'.

The idea is reenforced that you only, and grudgingly, cooperate with 'us' and you most certainly never do so with 'them.' An entirely unnecessary and unnatural disharmony is created based upon artificial groupings.

Of course I know there will be shouted against me that team sports are only a pale reflection of the cooperation needed by a tribe of hunters to snare their prey. Of course that is true. But it is also true that the prey need not be human beings! The minutest reflection will tell you how idiotic the concept of team sports is!

But once this concept of 'them and us' is introduced into the child, some very nasty things start to happen. The child's tolerance of others decreases, he or she thinks of him or herself as part of a small group of 'us' surrounded by hostile 'them.'

Let us move on.

EIGHT — EDUCATION FIVE

So there we have our poor child stranded in school being forced to learn hostility, even in the guise of loyalty. But the harm is deep-seated and permanent. Let us follow the course it takes.

The young person graduates into the world. He or she is already aware of his or her class in society, skin pigmentation, religion, nationality and so forth. Each of these divides the person from another group of human beings.

Those not belonging to the 'us' groups are different, are strangers, are, in a sense, inferior. The more this division has taken place the more fearful of strangers the person becomes. Loyalty to groups such as these—especially to the nation—is a highly prized social 'virtue.'

Under certain conditions these exclusive feelings can turn to genocide. Let me demonstrate.

The principal psychological characteristic of a social group to which one of your kind presently belongs is a feeling of superiority to other groups. Look, take an absurd, but actual, historical example. In old Constantinople there were two political parties, the Reds and the Greens.

Ideologically nothing separated them. They were composed of the same race of people. They followed the same religion. Their followers came from the same social backgrounds (the plebeians).

Yet these two parties engaged in vitriolic hate of each other, frequently leading to mass bloodshed (of course both parties were controlled by certain noble families who used them for their own ends, but that is immaterial to my argument). How absurd! (But cheering for your nation's hockey team is equally absurd.)

What happens if trouble breaks out within the territory of one of your nations? The group loyalty drilled into children results in their seeing their nation as superior to others. How can it then suffer from economic woes? hunger? crime? Obviously some other group is to blame.

The 'them' and 'us' of infancy has now led directly to the search for a scapegoat. It is the Jews, the blacks, the white males, the Muslims, the bourgeoisie, the 'them.' But, of course, they are inferior—weren't you taught in school that the other team was inferior? 'They' are to blame and if 'we' can punish them all will be well again.

Is the slaughter of six million Jews enough? Or 25 million Russian kulaks? Or a million Cambodians? Or 100,000 Iraqi soldiers? No. It is never enough. The slaughter, the racism, the torture will go on until the unprovable is proved—that your 'us' is better, more secure, than their 'us.' But we can change that.

NINE — EDUCATION SIX

I believe that I have demonstrated that we do not need a school to impart the kind of social mores that exist in your society, they are positively dangerous! Moreover, as we have seen, the school is the wrong place for the child to interact with either his peers or with other adults. So what is left?

Learning and dumping!

School, as is presently constituted, is the wrong place for the process of rekindling memory or, if you don't accept the theory of inherited memory, any other form of learning.

Look at your penitentiaries. Are they great centers of learning? No—then why should a school be? Education, to be effectual, must be voluntary. Oh! the howls of the educationalists against the very idea! But Yes! Yes! Yes! Voluntary!

Present the world to the child within the context of my kind of family. Let him or her gravitate to those adults who enthuse on certain subjects. And they will so gravitate! Some such adults will have a larger following than others, so be it. Let there be no fixed hours—the class can convene by mutual agreement (this will instill cooperation at an early age, and responsibility within a family setting). Above all let there be no compunction to attend, no examinations, no exclusions, no tests, no grades, no competitions—nothing to take the joy out of the experience. THIS IS EDUCATION!

The school, then, as one building, should be dead. Education should be spread throughout the family community.

Of course, this leaves the dumping ground. Ah, but I see you have seen my answer. Clever—I like you to be ahead of me. But just in case there are a few who do not 'get it,' let me tease the thing out to the end.

The dumping ground is based on the fact that your kind must go out to work and therefore you must 'keep the kids off the streets.' But what if work was voluntary? What if the need to eat and find shelter was divorced from the need to work? What if the need to work came from within—springing from the enthusiasm for certain subjects that the enthusiastic adults taught? What if child-minding was replaced by child-loving? Why should a child be excluded from anywhere? Would a father or a mother not relish the presence of a child at their workplace and the chance to instill their own enthusiasm into the child?

There, we have gotten rid of schools and developed education!

TEN — ANOTHER PAUSE

I am afraid I am going to take another pause before we go on. We have been going through some pretty tedious, though necessary, stuff, you and I.

I want to make the point again that you are innocent. All the disharmony in your mind is the result of forces that are, if not beyond your control, at least nothing of which you should feel in the least bit guilty.

I want to tell you, once again, that you are loved and that, if I have a message at all, it is that everything around you contributes to that love. Even when you feel hated by individuals, that hatred is only a perversion of love—distressing as that may be.

I want you to hold on to this love as we go forward and I want you to remember your innocence since that is the most fundamental thing that you have. It is as if you were still a baby and the world was still new—you were not born with guilt and you have no reason now for guilt or the self-hatred that goes with it.

And you are worthy of love, never forget that. No matter what the circumstances of your life, no matter to what depths society and your own inner demons have brought you—mentally, emotionally, economically, socially or spiritually—you are loved and you are worthy of love.

I will not allow any of my children to suffer unduly and, if they allow me, I will protect them from the more extreme ravages of their culture. I will not permit them to starve, I will not permit them to suffer the devastation of disease without the promise of relief and love.

That is my part of the bargain, if you like. I ask only one thing in return—self-acceptance and progress toward self-love.

I am not a maker of miracles and I do not, and cannot, alter the past. I cannot kill anything, even the deadliest virus. It too, is loved. Nor do I preach passive acceptance of your condition in life. Nor do I discount your will and the ability of your consciousness to affect all things around you.

What I offer is the love of All There Is and the shield that that love provides to those who accept it. Even when you rail against fate, that love will be there. Take it. When it is time for you to pass from this life, there will be my hand to greet your soul. When your children suffer, I will give you the power to protect them.

You are innocent. You are my children. I am but a small part of that love which rests there for you. All There Is and I beg for you to accept and love yourself. The universe, all universes, are created for one thing: love. Love is All There Is. Love yourself.

ELEVEN — FAMILIES AGAIN

If you have read and taken in all of the causes of your disharmony, and the problem with your education system, then you are now ready to move on. What is the next step? The next step is to see the future as it will be and find a place for your soul within it.

The future belongs to family-tribes as I have outlined them.

It may seem perverse, but I want to start with a negative—I want to start by saying what a family, in my view, is not:

It is not a 12-step program meeting in any of its many guises.

It is not an ashram.

It is not a neighborhood council.

It is not a genetic family.

It is not a commune.

All of these things may find their place within the family, but they cannot form the core of it. All are useful, but have one fatal flaw, as they are presently constituted: They are, each in their different way, exclusionary.

I know that this statement will be disputed, particularly by those who favor ashrams and 12-step programs. However, the 12-step program Alcoholics Anonymous, for example, is limited by its very nature to alcoholics. An ashram is limited by the kind of studies and meditation that take place within it. I know that this would take some more argument, but for the moment let it pass.

Another problem with all of these is that they are impermanent and that they have, with the exception of the commune and the 12-step program, a structured hierarchy. Many of them also suffer from the defect that they encourage membership by disharmonious people.

I first want to tackle the most important question regarding the creation of families—their practicality within your existing social system. Without an answer to this you will not follow me and nor will any other of your kind—and quite rightly so!

We are going to have to delve into the rather arcane worlds of finance and economics for a while.

Bear with me, I will be with you.

TWELVE — FAMILIES' ECONOMIC STRUCTURE

Economists among you are going to think me very simplistic for a while, but let that be. I am not writing a textbook.

Let us go into the world of economics as it is. In what you call the developed world there are two fundamental economic systems—one, the communist (or socialist) one, has gone into temporary decline. The other, the capitalist system, is foundering like an over-blown dysfunctional family. There is a lot of rhetoric devoted to the differences between these systems, but in essence they are the same.

Both depend on the notion that wealth is created by the addition of value to goods and services. Both would agree that the use of labor is one of the prime things that adds value—communists and socialists would lay more emphasis on labor, capitalists rather less.

Both allow for the concentration of wealth, capital, in a few hands, and, indeed, depend upon it for their survival. In the socialist view, the few hands consist of the state and its agencies whereas the capitalist system permits this concentration of wealth in the hands of private individuals. It is from these pools of wealth—state or private—that the financial resources needed for investment in plant, raw materials and labor (the wherewithal to add value) come.

It matters little to the worker in an auto plant whether his boss is General Motors or the state commission for automobiles. In most cases it is a boring, repetitive and thus disharmonious job anyway. Both state capital and private capital function alike. One may be more efficient than the other but, in terms of disharmony, both are identical.

There are, of course, gradations of both of these systems in the form of what are called 'mixed economies' such as are seen in most European countries. In these, however, the state plays a preeminent role in decision-making. Ultimately what they have created is a mix of state and private concentrations of economic power. To the worker in the auto plant this is just as unsatisfactory.

None of these systems work to create a harmonious society.

But the reasons for their failure lie deeper than the systems themselves, for they are merely symptoms. The ultimate cause of the failure is the economic relationships assumed between members of your kind.

I want to explore these in more depth now in order to explain how your kind got into this mess. Come, let us go on together.

THIRTEEN — FAMILIES' ECONOMIC STRUCTURE TWO

It is the assumption of 'value added' that is at the root of the failure of existing economic systems and their inability to bring harmony. In particular, it is their assumption that part of the added value lies in the labor content of the production of goods and services, that causes disharmony.

I see horror all around. 'But the value of labor is pivotal!' the cries go up. Wait, let us examine this a bit.

What do we mean by value? In its most simple form we mean something like this: A blacksmith buys metal from a mine (forgive my ignoring the steps in between the raw ore and the workable metal) and, using his strength and knowledge, fashions horse shoes and farm implements (Oh ATI! you're in another age!) which he then sells. The profit, to him, from this chain of transactions lies in the value that his skill has added to the raw metal. That is the theory.

At each stage—from the digging of the pit to the sale of the implements—some value has been added, so it goes. Each stage of added value depends on human skill, the assumption is made, whether the skill is that of the blacksmith, the miner, the mine owner or, in modern times, the computer programmer.

But is this really so? What actually happens, even in our simple example? And, again, what is really meant by value?

Let us first ask the question: Why? Why is the ore mined? Why are people prepared to give their 'value' to the mine owner? Why does the blacksmith make the horse shoes?

The obvious answer is that each needs money to purchase the necessities to survive. In essence, in your societies, that is true. But this motivation is only marginal to the theory of added value. Why? Because value, in labor terms, is defined (loosely) as the purchasing power, in goods and services, of a particular timespan of work, regardless of the motivation.

Of course, it is conceded that the motivation to earn the wherewithal to survive is crucial in persuading men to go down a pit or stare at a computer terminal. Now we are getting somewhere.

But what if we were to say that human value lies not in the act of labor, but in the fact of being. Your kind mouth platitudes about 'all men and women being equal' but the very notion of value at the heart of your system of economics depends on their being very much unequal. In a system of true equality, the economic motivation to go down the mine or sit before a screen would vanish because the worth of a human being would not depend on his or her economic activity.

It will be argued that I am confusing two meanings of the word 'value.' It will be said that value in economic terms and value in moral (or aesthetic or any other) terms are quite different and that the economic definition is narrowly confined to the production of goods and the provision of services.

I would reply by saying that it is the economists who do not realize what they are doing when they use the term and apply it to human labor. What they are doing is reducing the worth of a human being to the level of one factor in defining economic 'value.' Once you have done this then you can verbally treat humankind in the same way you would iron or electricity or any other of the nonsentient factors in the production process. Once you can do that verbally you can do it in reality—look at the starving people in many parts of the world who have been shut out of the 'added value' process. I would contend, very strongly, that the term value, even in the strict terms used by economists, is essentially a moral concept that reveals the hollowness of the whole theory of exchange.

Whether you give a person goods in exchange for his labor, or money, the net result is the same: You are valuing that person in material terms. The relationship is limited to the exchange of labor for materials. That is a pretty sorry relationship, and I would class it as wrong.

It is wrong because that is the wrong way to value any creature, and it is wrong because it short-changes the relationship. It puts a limit on the range of human interaction and is, in its very essence, disharmonious. I would stress that this is true whether we are talking about a barter system for the exchange of goods and labor or a monetary one. Money is only an intermediary barter.

The desire to work, or not to work, should be based on a variety of factors, none of which have anything to do with exchange. A person should work for the satisfaction of creating something—be it an automobile or a sculpture, or for the companionship of a jointly experienced workplace. The harmony created is the 'value.'

But is not the provider of the harmonious workplace entitled to a reward for providing it? Of course—the reward of bringing harmony to those within the workplace. But where is the motivation for entrepreneurship? For risk? To the extent that these bring harmony they have their own reward, to the extent that they do not they should not be practiced!

OH ATI—BE PRACTICAL!!

First let me hear you agree that, in an ideal world, what I have said would be true. Never mind, for the moment, the practicalities. Thank you. We are making progress.

FOURTEEN — FAMILIES' ECONOMIC STRUCTURE THREE

The practicalities, of course, are these:

There is a system of local, regional, national and international trade in place that will be difficult to dislodge.

There is no present way of existing in your society without making some economic contribution to the above system.

Your leaders refuse to think of alternatives, especially those alternatives that would deprive them of what they desire most—power.

Most people have an innate fear of change, particularly economic change.

I accept all this, and more, for there are far more practical difficulties than these. However, the above are the most ferocious roadblocks to the future. If we could get over these then the vision I have of a socially harmonious future would come easily to pass. It is therefore worth pursuing.

Most economists see trade: interregional, international, interstate as a good thing because it stimulates economic activity. I see it as quite the reverse. What it promotes is locality specialization, it robs areas of self-sufficiency and makes them dependent on goods from outside. It also makes people dependent on things happening outside their districts and outside their control. This dependency adds to their insecurity and thus to their disharmony. No amount of convenience or luxury or increase in the range of goods and services available can make up for this psychological damage.

It is hardly surprising that cultivation, the specialization of labor, money and urban living all happened at about the same time. The one inexorably leads to the other. At the same time social classes arose because there was now disposable wealth that could be accumulated and perpetuated in clans, families and guilds.

In order to restore harmony to economic relationships, a change must be made in the 'settled/urban/money' trading pattern.

I have said before that your kind are essentially hunter-gatherers and that for any social system to work, it must be compatible with the psychology of hunter-gatherers. If it is not it is doomed to fail. The present economic system is doomed because it is not compatible with the people you really are. That is what we must change.

FIFTEEN — FAMILIES' ECONOMIC STRUCTURE FOUR

hy, then, does the present system not work in favor of the hunter-gatherers that you fundamentally are? It is really quite simple, but first we must look at the economy of a hunter-gatherer society. It is not very complex. The essence of it is:

A lack of ownership.

A cooperative system of both hunting and gathering.

A sharing of the spoils of the hunt or the gather.

Self-sufficiency of the family group.

The lack of a division of labor (except between male and female, young and old).

There are other social factors concerning the structure of the family, tribal hierarchy and so forth that are important but for now it is the economics of the system (if that is what it can be called) that concern us.

I know it can be argued that another essence of the hunter-gatherers is that they are nomadic and that this, in itself, is an economic factor. Yes, but why are they nomadic? This is a vital point to be cleared up because it is obviously impossible for the entire population of the earth to take up nomadism.

Hunter-gatherers were nomadic because they followed the migration of their principal prey—whether it was the Lapps following the reindeer or the Plains Indians following the bison. In other words the economic prod toward being nomadic lay in the hoofs of the grazing animals they slaughtered for food and skins. Hunter-gatherers would have been settled if their prey had been settled and if the roots that they foraged for were plentiful enough.

Now back to essentials. If we must construct an economic system that is compatible with hunter-gatherers, we must incorporate those features which I have detailed above.

But there is another, more fundamental, objection that we must deal with first. According to this, humankind became hunter-gatherers merely because that was the most efficient method of obtaining food—in other words, for economic reasons. If that is so then any change to another system for economic reasons—to settled agriculture and husbandry for example—is just as 'natural' since it is merely an adaption to another system.

The argument begs two questions that we must now deal with: Why did your kind become hunter-gatherers? What is involved in any adaptation to a new system? Come, now it gets interesting.

SIXTEEN — FAMILIES' ECONOMIC STRUCTURE FIVE

Why did you become hunter-gatherers? Was it because humans saw the economic advantages of hunter-gathering and took it up? Or was it because they evolved so that they could take advantage of the system?

The distinction is subtle but important. If it was the former then your kind could readily adapt to any system but, if it was the latter, then far stronger and more deep-rooted influences are at work that inhibit such easy adaptation.

You evolved from simian ancestors who were primarily gatherers. Over a period of five million years those ancestors gradually evolved to take advantage of a more varied diet which included meat-eating. (I am going to ignore the fact that some of the modern great apes—particularly chimpanzees—do, occasionally, eat meat and that others, for example the bonobos, make tools. An entire book would be needed to explain the evolutionary forces at work within those species that led to these behavior patterns.)

For this purpose they began to stand upright, for this

purpose their hands evolved into tool-fashioning and-using implements, for this purpose their brains expanded (and new minds were added, but that controversial point I will leave aside), since catching their prey required more thought and planning.

Each stage in evolution was directed at only one objective—to make your kind better hunters and, with tools, more efficient gatherers.

So, some five million years elapsed between the first tentative attempts at a more varied diet and modern man. This being so, it can easily be seen that the process of adaptation to the 'new' system involved the evolution of a whole new species. And if this is the case then your kind is still a hunter-gathering species since it has not materially changed since Cro-Magnon and Neanderthal man, both of whom were hunter-gatherers.

Now, to follow this point home: You cannot divorce an economic system from human evolution. Humankind will remain a hunter-gathering species until, many millions of years from now, they evolve to take advantage of another way of life.

To try and impose anything else leads directly to disharmony—as all of the experiments in other systems have shown. Therefore whatever system we construct must be compatible with the species that you are.

Does this mean going back to the bush and living the life of a 'primitive?' No, of course not. But it does mean rethinking your entire present socioeconomic system from the bottom up. I use that last phrase on purpose because up to now systems have been imposed from the top down. ATI is not a dictator!

SEVENTEEN — FAMILIES' ECONOMIC STRUCTURE SIX

So, if you are still hunter-gatherers, you must have an economic and social structure appropriate to hunter-gatherers.

To a hunter-gatherer the idea of ownership—private or state—is foreign.

To a hunter-gatherer the only division of labor is between young and old, male and female.

Their system is cooperative rather than competitive.

Any one of these will rule out any existing economic structure as inappropriate and therefore disharmonious. Yet, as I have said, problems exist: There are far more of your kind now, and you have advanced technologically even as you have regressed socially.

A technological civilization requires a high degree of education and specialization in order to survive, it is argued. From this simple base premise the whole paraphernalia of the state can be argued into being. It is therefore wrong.

It is wrong because of the meanings normally attached to the words 'education' and 'specialization.' Education, as practiced in your societies, is extremely disharmonious—as I believe I have shown. If the system of education was to become as I have outlined earlier, then 'specialization' would happen naturally as a result.

But it would not be the sort of specialization that you have now. In your present societies you generally work at a particular profession or trade because you have to. You enter a trade or profession because you perceive that there will be a market for your acquired skills. Of course, if there is not that market you are discarded and made to feel useless and a burden on the state or your family or whatever.

In a cooperative society this feeling would be unknown. The absurdity of the present way can be shown thus: You work to earn money; you spend the money on goods and services; in order to create those goods and services others go to work; the society becomes dependent on the spending; but in order to be profitable an enterprise must economize on labor; if it uses less labor it creates less wealth; if less wealth is created fewer goods are made; if fewer goods are made less people can work; if there is no work for you to do, you cannot spend money on goods and services and they will not be created; the enterprises will not start and so forth and so forth. It is a continuous merry-go-round. In the end, you are a mere consumer in a society that has no direction other than production and that is doomed to collapse.

EIGHTEEN — ANOTHER INTERMISSION

I want to take a little time to explain a bit further something about myself. My child Bob, in his private sessions with people, is often asked 'But what is Ati?' He tells them that I am a link between him and All There Is, which is true. He says that I have never lived, and that is true. But it is all very unsatisfactory.

I am an event defining itself. I see that you think that this is even less satisfactory. What on earth does it mean?

A persona such as myself is an event that happens when a soul is created. As such, I have no physical existence at all. It is said that at the center of a black hole there is an event without physical form and that that event has so much power that it draws matter toward it. Eventually all nearby matter is sucked into the black hole and becomes part of the event. Since the event has such power, no light or other energy of any kind can escape from it, so it is optically invisible.

Of course all that analogy says is that an event can have presence without physical being. It can have power without that power being visible.

So a nonphysical event being 'real' is not too hard to

grasp in the light of your present understanding of astrophysics, but what about 'defining itself'? The center of a black hole is not conscious, I am. My consciousness comes from the Universal Consciousness, the mind, if you like, within which all things exist. That consciousness is forever expanding—creating itself, defining itself in terms of what it creates.

In the same way, I expand through all the lives that the soul I accompany lives. I am defined by those existences, and I help create their scope. By those existences I am self-discovered.

At the same time I am linked to the Universal Consciousness. I am, if you like, one of the eyes through which it sees creation and I form part of the means of its self-definition.

As I expand, I increase in love. Love is an essential part of my self-definition.

Oh dear, am I losing you? And I wanted to be so clear. Well, I feel better. It is difficult, sometimes, to be a being that is essentially untranslatable into your languages. Perhaps it is best if I remain just Ati.

NINETEEN — THE REVOLUTION

I feel better. My minutiae aren't important anyway. Now let us go forward.

There are an awful lot of things that your society produces, with its fine, efficient means of production, that are useless. I shall name a very few:

Automobiles, jets, washing machines, toothpaste, super-highways, submachine guns, luxury liners, whiskey, cigarettes, subways, tanks, video cameras, law journals, sleeping pills, antidepressant drugs, school buildings, prisons, hamburgers etcetera etcetera.

All of them are produced to allow enterprises to make work, none produces even the smallest bit of harmony—not to the worker in the factory making them, not to the owner of the factory, not to the taxpayer subsidizing their manufacture, not to the creative minds used to advertise them or to the not-so-creative minds running the enterprises.

You need so little for harmony—love, adequate shelter, health, food, freedom and community. Automobiles and jets take you away from community, washing machines cause isolation, a soft twig is better than toothpaste, if you do not have cars you do not need super-highways, if you have community you do not need submachine guns or tanks, cigarettes, prisons or whiskey or all the rest.

If you do not have to create what you do not need then many of the skills you now prize will be seen to be needless—advertising, policing (the function of the police is, very largely, to prevent people stealing what they do not need from people who do not need the stolen articles. What idiocy!), production managers, lawyers (lawyers largely seek to define who owns which useless article and which law should apply to its ownership. What absurdity!) and so forth.

The results of specialization, to the absurd extent that you have it, are entirely disharmonious.

It follows that if you can do without all these mass-produced and labor-intensive items, you do not need a society large enough to organize their production or an education system geared to produce the skills to facilitate their manufacture.

In fact you do not need a society as you know it at all. This is the essence of my social revolution—the literal destruction of your society. There are choices to be made—there is a trade-off between the security, love, freedom and community I offer and the ownership and production of goods for their own sakes. It is not an easy choice. No, really, it is difficult.

First you need to know how a family would actually work. Now we get to the heart of the matter. Follow me, children.

TWENTY — MY FAMILY

First let me state a truism—you are all my family. You all have my love and the love of All There Is. You are all part of the divine and you all have a place on this planet and a role to play upon it. There is not one of you who ought to be made to feel in any way separated from that love and that sense of belonging.

I have said that a human family should be somewhere between the size of a village and a small town. It does not matter that the numbers be exactly the same, but there should be sufficient people to carry out the tasks needed for the continuation of the family and the rearing of its children, and yet not so many that you need a formal governmental organization.

A child will grow up in this family knowing the whole adult community as its role-models and a great many of them as its teachers and its mentors. He or she will thus be in harmony with the family in a way no present human child is.

The young person's interests will be drawn toward one or more of the functions that the family needs or enjoys. He or she will not be excluded because of his or her lack of 'ability' because ability will have been honed through interest. And anyway a family can afford to have those of unequal talents accepted as a right.

The person may marry and, possibly, have children. These offspring will be the responsibility of the community at large and will be happily accepted as such.

All persons—adult or child—will have an equal say in the running of the family and no decision will be taken except by consensus. If this means no decisions are taken, so be it. ('Oh come now, Ati! What about emergencies?' Oh! Because all of the family are in harmony with one another, they will act together in emergencies and the minority will willingly go along with the majority. How could you possibly think otherwise?)

There will be no private ownership as such—not land, not buildings, not goods. But each individual will have such security that ownership is not relevant. For example: What does it matter who owns the house you live in, provided there is no danger of it being taken away from you? You only own to secure, if you are secure you need not own.

Then to whom does the house belong? Nobody. The family will undertake the building of sufficient houses (or whatever form of shelter its members want) for itself but will not own them. Remember what I said about ownership and the hunter-gatherers.

Since there is no ownership there is no need for money; a person's worth springs from his being. 'Oh, Ati, you're being idealistic again!' Yes, of course, and practical. Come.

TWENTY-ONE — INTER-FAMILY TRADE

amilies will interact with each other and will cooperate with each other and will engage in a form of trade.

'But if there is no ownership, how can there be trade?'

The very question shows that you are still wedded to the idea of owning goods. In the way you organize commerce at the moment, it is assumed that goods are passed from one owner to another and that the privilege of ownership is conferred in return for money or other goods.

Look, family A makes a car for its own use. It is used by all the members of the family according to their desire or need. If they build a second car, perhaps the first will be redundant. Family B needs a car. Well then, let them use it. Ask for nothing in return. The harmony generated on both sides by the transaction is sufficient reward in itself. You have not transferred ownership because there never was any.

In a similar way, if then or at some other time, family A needs medical supplies, family B will make them available—not in return for the car, but for the harmony produced.

You will recall that the main goal of each member of any family is their own and the family's harmony. Trade evolves into the act of giving and receiving harmony. But never to the point where one family is dependent on others for anything except the odd emergency or incidentals.

'But isn't giving a transference of ownership?' Yes, but only if there is an assumed ownership in the first place. It is difficult because your language has no adequate word for this 'freely making available' that I am discussing.

The point is that in these transactions there is no assumption of ownership.

'What if the car is not made available, but stolen?' For what purpose would you steal the car? You would not be able to repair it, fuel it or perhaps transport it, without the support network that a family provides. Further, an item is stolen, in your present society, mostly in order to resell it. If there are no buyers and no medium of exchange—money—to consummate the sale there would be little point in stealing anything.

'But what of land? What if one family is forcefully dispossessed by another?' This is a crucial question because without the basic security of a home no person will be persuaded that a family such as I am advocating is a good idea. For the moment I am going to duck the question. But we will come back to it. First let us continue with automobiles!

TWENTY-TWO — AUTOMOBILES

I do not like automobiles; there are better and more pleasurable ways to travel that do not cause massive pollution and do not kill. Automobiles kill not only by their crashes but also by the way the roads are made—so many trees per mile, so many blades of grass, so many birds' nests. These are the prices your kind pays for this ungainly contraption.

But, if a family wants one, so be it. However, the fact of a car relies on a whole host of assumptions—that it can be made, that fuel is available, that there are roads, that there are distances worth using it for.

If it is to be made, it must be made by the members of the family. There will be no factories, no Detroit in America or Luton in England, where these things are churned out. If there are enough people in the family with the skills, or enough people with the enthusiasm to learn the skills, then automobiles will be created.

The monster will be serviced if there is someone within the group who is enthusiastic enough to do the work. It will be fuelled if a member can be found who can create the fuel, and wants to do so. It will be used by anyone who wants to use it. When they have finished they will leave it with the keys in it for someone else to take. Cambridge, in England, had a similar system with bicycles. Very few went missing, even when bicycles were worth money!

If the family is spread over a wide area (where the land is poor for example) then it may be that many cars are made and men or women will decide to make servicing them their full-time occupation.

If the family decides that the vehicles should be left in a central car-pool, then most people will go along with that. If they do not, they will not be fined or imprisoned. The punishment will be the disharmony the rule-breaker feels at being out of line with his or her fellows.

Of course the same is true of any other decisions of the family. Remember that no rule can be brought in without the full, or at least tacit, consent of all the members. To go against such a ruling would make the offender feel very isolated and the offense would probably not last long.

As it is with automobiles, so it is with every single good or service the family utilizes. Without ownership there would be no waste. The law of supply and demand would still be operative, but the means of producing and distributing the goods would be completely different.

Take a while to understand this, and then follow me if you will.

TWENTY-THREE — THE WHOLE FAMILY

So there you have it, the family. It is no impossible Utopia, it works because it is natural that it should work, because it treats people like the parts of the divine that they are. It works because it has none of the destructive divisions that your present society has to cope with.

There are, within it, no divisions of wealth or power or prestige based on anything except utility to the family. You cannot buy anything, especially human labor. Yet there is no diminution of your standard of living: What you need, you have.

There is, however, one last problem that we must turn to. What if one family is forcefully dispossessed of its land by another? What if there is aggression? What if the material resources of one family become exhausted and they turn, perhaps in desperation, upon the lands of another? What, in other words, is the ultimate security?

At first sight there are a multitude of problems associated with every solution to this most basic dilemma. Yet without some guarantee of security, the families will not come into existence.

But there is an answer.

The answer lies in the question of ownership. A naked man in the desert will not be harmed (except by the sun or a venomous snake!) or robbed. Why? Because there is nothing to take. He owns nothing. A family owns nothing. When the starving members of the invading family arrive they will be absorbed, their skills utilized, their disharmonies cured.

'Oh, Ati!'

Yes! And even if there are millions of people on the move, the very smallness and integrity of each family will prevent wholesale social disruption to the receiving families. There is nothing to steal, nothing to take. More houses will be built, more corn grown—the supply will meet the demand. For a while you may have two, or more, families living in the same geographic territory.

'But won't this amalgam become a nation? Won't the whole wretched business begin again?'

No! The traditions of leaderlessness and lack of ownership are the very antithesis of the nation-state. Think about it. How could an aggressive nation arise if there were no prizes to fight for, if there were no leaders to lead, no followers to follow and no boundaries to be fought over? In a sense every man is the naked man in the desert (or woman, if you prefer). But.......

TWENTY-FOUR — SECURITY

But.............you are all hunter-gatherers! The essence of a hunter-gatherer is to move when times are hard to a place where they are not so bad. Look at the Mexicans trying to cross the United States border now! Look at the Russian Jews fleeing to Israel. Look at the masses of refugees in all parts of the world.

Security can only come through the willingness to absorb, to acknowledge the hunter-gatherer within you and your fellows.

'We will be overrun!' Nonsense. The Roman Empire lasted for half a millennia by absorbing tribes who crossed over its borders. If the United States got rid of its borders and allowed the Mexicans to enter what would happen? There would be an infusion of the youngest and most determined of people who would add enormously to the wealth of the overall population.

There is a difference between migration and conquest, a difference not understood by your kind. You see the Mexicans or whatever as a conquering mass, not as a reservoir of talent to be welcomed. A Mexican family arriving in San Diego does not want to take the house of a resident, but to build it's own.

If the arrival of all these immigrants means that the area has become too overburdened with people, then some will move on and the population will even out. I tell you that the Sahel, the area just south of the Sahara, was not made into a semi-desert by climate, but by the fact that the people there could not move to better pastures when the land could no longer support their goats—it was the fact of impenetrable international boundaries that turned a fertile region into an arid one. The climatic shift happened later as the earth tried to rid itself of humans in that area so it could heal.

North Africa was the bread basket of the Mediterranean before the natural shift of peoples was prevented by false restrictions.

Politics comes first and climate follows—the exact opposite of what most of your kind imagines! The desert is a healing thing, preparing the way for later fertility—like a scar on a wound. You know the old saying—leave the scar alone!

So that is your ultimate security, freedom of movement!

Oh! I know that many of you will not see this at first, the fear of change is so great. The fear for your possessions, for your house, for the land of your birth or adoption. But you, in reality, own none of these things. None of them! The only security you can have is in the type of family I am leading you toward, and freedom, absolute freedom. All I want to give you, my children, is the freedom to be. To be a part of All There Is, to be at one with your neighbors, to feel connected to everyone and everything as part of your own body, and soul.

There is one last objection that I see in your minds. What if you and your fellows form a family and give up all the safety—such as it is—of the present social system, and no one else does? Would you not then be just an isolated island in a sea of hostility, a prey to all the regulations of the nation-state and to the envy and predacious behavior of those members still living under the 'old' system?

This objection assumes that you are going to start a fully-fledged family at once overnight. That will not happen. As I said earlier, the families will start and will have to work out a <u>modus vivendi</u> with the existing order. As the number of family-tribes escalates, the apparatus of the state becomes irrelevant. For this to happen may take generations.

But, you ask, if it is not going to happen in my lifetime, why should I start? The answer is simple—what have you got to lose? Would you rather travel to harmony in the company of other like-minded people or would you rather sink into the abyss of your present society? Many, through fear of the unknown, will genuinely choose the latter. As I said earlier, love them and let them go.

For those who want to begin this trek into your future, come with me, I will lead you and I will keep you safe. Come for the love of All There Is. Come for the love of your fellows and immediate families. Come for the love of your planet. Come for the love of yourselves. Come for the love of me. You are my children.

TWENTY-FIVE — THE SONG OF ALL THERE IS

I am the Earth beneath your feet
And your shoes.
I am the blade of grass that bends
And is broken by your step.
I am the joy you feel
And your sorrow.
And the day you know
And tomorrow.

I am the food upon your plate
And the living thing that died
To make it.
I am the watch you use to count the hours
And every second counted.
I am the eyes that watch and count
And the event
You rush toward.
I am the very question why
And I give the answer
I.

I am the sky you look toward
The sun, the constellations.
I am the warmth you feel in spring
And the cold of dying.
I am the love you feel
And your lover.
I am the tree which gives you fruit
And cover.

I am All There Is, I am the One,
And I am the many.
I am all the things you want to be
I am all the things you were.
I am the arms you come to—
Ever open.
I am you, I am you.
Your every part, and your whole.
I am All There Is and I am
Your soul.

Peace my children.

This ends the first book of Ati, Persona.

A WEEK OF DAILY AFFIRMATIONS

AFFIRMATION FOR THE FIRST DAY

Today I will acknowledge my own importance. I will say, boldly, that I am the most important person in my life.

I will see that, as an important person, I have the right to my own feelings, my own thoughts and my own needs. I will carefully monitor my thoughts, my actions and my words to make sure that they confirm to this newly-affirmed importance.

I will realize that each negative thought concerning myself is part of the programming from my past and part of the pattern I wish to break. I will not accept others' remarks if they are disparaging of me. I will not say things that tend to put me down. I will ask myself before each action: Is this what an important person would do? Before each utterance: Is this what an important person would say? After each thought: Is this what an important person would think?

Today I will acknowledge my own importance.

AFFIRMATION FOR THE SECOND DAY

Today I will be one with All There Is. I will allow myself to see beauty in all things.

I will be able to see past my own narrow concerns, escape my own rigidity. I will look for harmony: harmony in nature and in people. I will allow myself to smile, even at strangers, and I will enjoy the smiles I get in return.

I will take time to notice the complexity of All There Is and yet revel in its simple beauty. I will let the wind pass over my face like the hand of a loving mother. I will notice subtle colors and different bird calls, even in the midst of a large city.

Above all I will find beauty in myself. I am part of the All There Is that I now see as beautiful, complex and loving. I will permit myself to savor each moment of this day.

I will not allow the pain and suffering I have felt to intrude upon this day.

Today I will be one with All There Is.

AFFIRMATION FOR THE THIRD DAY

Today I will feel the love of All There Is. I will feel loved and protected by each tree, each bird, each blade of grass. I will become aware that the entire universe is founded on love and that love is there for me to share.

Because I feel this love I can accept. I can accept the frailties within myself and within others. My love will no longer be blocked, or given grudgingly as a reward, or held out tantalizingly just out of the reach of others.

In my family there may have been promises not kept, fear, anger and guilt. Love may have been fractured by confused thoughts, addiction, helplessness. But today all that is gone, like the clouds that break after days of rain, clearing my sky. I shall no longer dwell on the pain of the past.

Today I will feel the love of All There Is and cleanse my soul in that love.

AFFIRMATION FOR THE FOURTH DAY

Today I give myself the peace of All There Is. I am at one with my God and feel that presence in everything. It is this feeling that gives me the ability to slow down, to be calm.

I will not get caught in the activity trap caused by shame and guilt. I will not try to find things to do in order to escape from myself. Instead I will find peace within myself. I will take time to listen instead of talk; time to sit and stare at the rhythm of nature rather than at the frenetic activity of others who are also trying to escape from themselves.

In slowing down my physical pace, I will slow down emotionally. I will not be sucked into others' emotional wilderness but will allow myself the luxury of choosing my own feelings.

Above all I will find that peace which is the consciousness of All There Is. I am a child of God, I can have peace.

AFFIRMATION FOR THE FIFTH DAY

Today I will allow myself to seek new opportunities. In the past I have been held back by anxiety, by the sense that I am bound to fail.

I recognize that this is rooted in my past, in my inability to save my parents from their alcoholism, their depression, their anger. I see that a child cannot save its parents.

I now free myself from the guilt associated with this imagined failure. I will eagerly seek out new avenues in my work, and new relationships in my personal life. Nothing and nobody can hold me back.

I can succeed in whatever I set out to do. When new opportunities arise I will be ready for them. I am in control of my own life and will remain so from today forth.

Today I will allow myself to say yes to opportunity. I will not be afraid, I will not let anxiety stop me.

AFFIRMATION FOR THE SIXTH DAY

Today I will take stock of my friendships. I will look at each person and ask: Do they give me importance and attention? Are they there for me or am I only there for them?

I will pretend that I am starting a tribe of harmonious, cooperative, people. I will select those from among my acquaintances whom I would want to have as part of my tribe. I will not be afraid to exclude those who are my blood relatives, even my parents, if they are not harmonious. I will ask: How close is this person to a oneness with All There Is? Can I benefit from his or her harmony?

I will not select people for what they do, but for who they are and how they act toward me.

I will begin to structure my relationships on this tribal pattern. I will put myself at the center of my tribe and seek harmony in the company of others.

AFFIRMATION FOR THE SEVENTH DAY

Today I imagine I am in a place of light. At first I see nothing else around me because the light is so strong. Slowly I begin to realize that I am not alone in this place of light. There is a tree standing beside me. I reach out and touch it, it gives me strength.

There is a child there, who is me. I embrace the child and we exchange love. The child in me takes me by the hand and shows me the love of All There Is. I am no longer nothing, I am the child of All There Is.

I realize that as a part of this creation I can never be alone, that I can draw strength and support from everything around me.

I wait for a while savoring that love and support, building up my self-reliance and strength. Now I am ready for the day.

MY OWN AFFIRMATION

MY OWN AFFIRMATION TWO

INDEX

L

N

P

R

S

T

U

V

W

ALSO AVAILABLE FROM EUROPEAN AMERICAN PUBLISHING

MONOGRAPHS BY ATI

Affirmation to All There Is $5
On the nature of the divine and how you can come to union with All There Is.

Child Rearing $5
How to bring up a child in harmony. A practical guide to the crucial early years of childhood.

Death $5
A detailed look at what happens just before death, at death and the experience of the soul after death.

Healing $5
What it means to be a healer. How to become a healer. The difference between healing and curing. The why of illness and suffering.

Mastering Your Personal Power $5
How to take your power back from external authorities and free yourself from internalized, negative, programming.

Science and the Spirit $5
A look at the relationship between science and spirituality.

Each monograph is approximately 15-20 pages long and is loose bound.

CASSETTE AUDIO TAPES BY ATI

Innocence/The Journey $9.95
Perhaps the last and most powerful self-help tool you'll ever need. You can rescue your inner child and banish guilt forever. *The Journey* is a guided meditation for deep relaxation and an expanded consciousness.

Just a Minute $9.95
Thirty-one short, practical, yet deeply spiritual daily affirmations. Start each day of the month out right.

COMING SOON IN 1995!

ATI: FROM BIRTH TO DEATH
Ati's sccond book delves more deeply into the nature of the soul, death and reincarnation, the reality of God, pain and suffering, child rearing how to make ideal relationships and much more.

FELDENKRAIS® TAPES

A series of audio cassette tapes prepared for *EAP* by Alicia Fortinberry, one of America's best-known Feldenkrais practitioners, lecturer, writer and TV personality. The tapes gently teach each part of the body to move with ease and grace.

Inner Moves $9.95
A powerful 'somatic meditation' to eliminate stress entirely. On side two, a really effective and gentle exercise to alleviate back pain.
Empower Your Body $19.95

Six Awareness Through Movement® exercises to dramatically improve and revitalize every part of yourself.

Feldenkrais® Exercises for the Physically Impaired $19.95
Six ATM exercises for those suffering from MS, strokes, back and other injuries. Many can be performed in a wheelchair.

For all orders, add $1.50 for postage and handling within the U.S.
Nevada residents add the appropriate sales tax.

To : EUROPEAN AMERICAN PUBLISHING
Please rush me ....copies of the following titles:
1...
2...
3...
4...
☐ *My check for $...........made out to European American Publishing*
☐ *Please charge my VISA/MasterCard*
#...Expiration date..................
☐ *I don't wish to order now, but please put me on your mailing list for news of forthcoming titles.*
Name...
Address...
..State..
.....Zip............
Send to:European American Publishing, Dept.A, 1280 Terminal Way, Suite 3, Reno, NV 89502. Allow 6 weeks for delivery.